The Language of Wings

BobWhite

Books by the Author

(*with Denver Bryan)

The Language of Wings

—ESSAYS ON WATERFOWL—

E. Donnall Thomas Jr.

Photographs by Don and Lori Thomas

Raven's Eye Press
Durango, Colorado

Raven's Eye Press
Durango, Colorado
www.ravenseyepress.com

Thomas, Jr., E. Donnall.
   The Language of Wings: Essays on Waterfowl/E. Donnall Thomas, Jr.
   p. cm.

1. Hunting
2. Travel
3. Adventure
4. Wildlife
I. Title

ISBN: 978-0-9816584-9-0
LCCN: 2011934002

Cover & interior design by Lindsay J. Nyquist, *elle jay design*
Cover art by Bob White, www.bobwhitestudio.com
All photography by Don & Lori Thomas

Printed in the United States of America
1 3 5 7 9 10 8 6 4 2

Table of Contents

I. WATERFOWL

II. IN THE FIELD: DUCKS

III. In the Field: Geese and Beyond

IV. Retrievers

V. THE WATERFOWLING CULTURE

Late season on a spring fed Montana slough.

Acknowledgements

THE MATERIAL IN Chapters 37, 38, 39, 44, 45, 48, 66, 69, and 72 has not been published previously, nor has the introductory essay at the beginning of each of the five text segments. In different form, Chapter 19 appeared in *Alaska*, Chapter 59 in *Retriever Journal* and Chapter 47 in *Just Labs*. The remaining chapters come from Closing Time columns in *Ducks Unlimited* magazine, plus an occasional modified feature from the same magazine.

I wish to express my appreciation to the entire DU staff, with special thanks to editors Tom Fulgham and Matt Young. I also appreciate the invaluable contributions made by Lindsay Nyquist of elle jay design, Ken Wright of Raven's Eye Press, and cover artist Bob White. Finally, gratitude goes to my wife Lori Thomas for her role in the photography and manuscript preparation, among a great many other things. Without their support, this project would not have been possible.

Incoming! Yellow-billed pintails in Argentina.

Dedication

THIS BOOK IS DEDICATED TO the late Chuck Petrie. A warm, affable man with boundless enthusiasm for wildlife and wild places, Chuck enriched the lives of countless members of the outdoor community, and his support for my writing proved crucial time and again. His untimely death in 2005 left a huge void, but his many friends will always remember him at closing time.

Setting up on the Columbia.

Foreword

I HAVE NEVER HAD THE PLEASURE of meeting Don Thomas in person, but like his other faithful readers, I feel I know him well from what he has written. As an editor of Ducks Unlimited magazine, I have had the great privilege of previewing some of his finest work. He has written our back page column, Closing Time, for a decade, and as our field editor also regularly writes feature articles on a variety of topics pertaining to waterfowl. I am delighted that he has collected many of these stories and others in this book, so they may be enjoyed by his many fans—old and new alike—for years to come.

      One doesn't have to read much of the author's writing to realize that he has a different perspective than many of his contemporaries. The son of a Nobel laureate, he's a third-generation physician who received a degree in English before attending medical school and specializing in internal medicine. Writing consistently at a high level is never easy, but he makes his craft look as effortless as anyone I know. A few times every year we discuss concepts for potential stories and then agree on assignments for future issues of the magazine—typically months in advance. Invariably his flawless manuscripts will arrive via e-mail long before they're due with a short note that says something like, "I was rained in at camp, so I thought I would get ahead on a few assignments..." If only all writers could be so efficient!

Like other great writers, the author is a born storyteller, and he lives a life that provides plenty of interesting material to write about. How many outdoor writers have taken big game on five continents with a longbow, piloted a bush plane to a duck shack on Cook Inlet tide flats, guided brown bear hunters on the Alaska Peninsula, and made seviche for friends from a redfish caught in the Gulf of Mexico? All of this and much more appear to come naturally to him, just like his ability to describe his outdoor adventures in lyrical prose. But I believe the author is at his best when he writes about the common experiences shared by waterfowlers everywhere: the cherished company of family and friends, the sights and sounds of a duck marsh at dawn, the joys of hunting with a faithful retriever, the satisfaction of making a good, clean shot, and the endless mysteries of waterfowl and the natural world.

I'm certain that you will treasure this wonderful collection of waterfowl hunting stories as much as I do. Here is a book by an author who could have written about a great many subjects. We are truly fortunate that he chose to devote his time and talent to writing about our favorite things.

Matt Young
Memphis, Tennessee

Preface

LIKE MOST FREELANCE WRITERS in the field, my internal computer has been programmed to function in blocks of 2500 words. That's the length of the typical outdoor magazine feature, and after producing over 1000 of them in the last 20 years, my verbal thought processes gravitate toward that format almost as a matter of instinct.

Hence my initial trepidation when Chuck Petrie contacted me in 2001 about doing a new back page column for Ducks Unlimited magazine. Each piece had to be 800 words, right on the money. Was it really possible to say anything meaningful about a subject as rich and complex as waterfowl in such constrained space?

Of course it was...Hemingway once observed that all bad writers are in love with the epic, while E. B. White advised young writers: "When in doubt, cut it out." I like to think that the discipline and focus Chuck's vision demanded eventually made me a better writer. It certainly made me a better editor.

It also subtly altered the way I regard the subject matter. Perhaps more than any other undertaking in the field, waterfowling invites enthusiasm for the grand spectacle, as openly acknowledged in several of the essays that follow. But ducks and geese and their pursuit ultimately involve so much more. The short column format allowed me to examine the bricks as well as the building, and the insights that followed left me with an enhanced appreciation of the wild world outside.

An appreciation I can now only hope to share.

Don Thomas
Lewistown, Montana

Section I

Waterfowl

Hen mallard on the wing.

Waterfowl

THE FAMOUS MARTIAL DICTUM about the importance of knowing the enemy sounds harsh when applied to the pursuit of waterfowl, fascinating and admirable wild creatures with which I cannot imagine an adverse relationship. So let's rephrase and advise to know the quarry instead.

As indeed most serious duck and goose hunters do. Hunting and the study of natural history go hand in hand. A career in the field provides an opportunity for the kind of observation-based firsthand knowledge no bird book or ornithology course can provide. Ask for a quick ID on an inbound flight of puddle ducks in low light, and I'll trust the guy wearing the duck call around his neck over the birder with the binoculars and field guide any day.

Of course, attaching names to specimens properly offers but part of the challenge… and the reward. The duck blind perspective provides a backstage pass to the world of waterfowl as few others will ever know it. I don't think it's much of a stretch to invoke the concept of intimacy: the myriad of shared secrets that distinguish certain relationships from all the rest. That defines the way duck hunters know ducks.

I've hunted ducks in a lot of different places. Here in North America, the birds themselves provide a common thread running between remarkably diverse waterfowling destinations. Whether the decoys are set up in a Texas Gulf coastal marsh or a tundra pothole on the Alaska Peninsula, the cast of characters will largely be the same. Of course that observation reflects the birds' migratory nature; they are among the few wildlife species that get around as much as I do. Away from home, the quarry's familiarity breeds a certain reassurance. A mallard is a mallard, in all four flyways.

I was fortunate enough to grow up in an environment that emphasized the ideal unity between hunter and naturalist right from the start. Waterfowl and game birds were always more than feathered targets around our house, to be studied and appreciated as well as shot. It didn't take me long to appreciate that the learning was every bit as important as the shooting. Decades later, I note that waterfowlers endorse this principle more consistently than any other group of hunters I know, an observation that should make them proud.

All of which easily becomes muddled nowadays, given contemporary standards of political correctness in the outdoors. "Non-consumptive users of wildlife" disdain hunters because we sometimes kill what we all love, never mind that without organized efforts from the hunting community there would be no birds for the watchers to watch. How much wiser it would be to make the squabbling stop and move on to the common defense of wildlife against the real enemies: irresponsible development, misuse of public lands, pollution, and other threats to wildlife habitat too numerous to mention.

But enough of that… I've always made a lousy politician, which is probably why I prefer the company of Labrador retrievers to most people. Time to move on to what really matters: the birds, viewed from a waterfowler's perspective.

Drake shoveler in breeding plumage.

Rocky with a drake wood duck.

CHAPTER ONE

The Eye of the Beholder

ONE REALLY COULDN'T SAY that dawn broke that dreary January morning. Thanks to a dense layer of fog shrouding the Columbia basin, daylight arrived almost imperceptibly, as if higher powers were toying with a celestial rheostat. But eventually dark shapes materialized overhead to accompany the chorus of wings we'd been listening to, and after consultation with his watch, my father announced the arrival of legal shooting light.

The first birds to settle into the spread were pintails, which we'd previously agreed not to shoot because their numbers were down that year. A lone mallard drake followed them and my father dropped him smoothly, affording Rocky a chance to release some restrained canine enthusiasm after the long drive from Montana. Due at the plate for the next single, when a lone bird appeared from the gloom a few minutes later I shifted into shooting position and concentrated on making a positive identification.

Larger than a teal but smaller than anything else we'd seen that morning, the new arrival's silhouette and flight pattern triggered an odd flood of distant memories. Finally, a realization clicked and the shock of recognition almost made me forget to shoot. But a childhood's worth of tutelage courtesy of the grizzled figure sitting beside me in the blind had left me too well trained for that. At the shotgun's report, the bird folded neatly and I settled back to let Rocky deliver the first wood duck I'd killed in years.

Back when I was growing up in the Atlantic Flyway, woodies were an everyday autumn staple. In response to concerns about loss of habitat, everyone was building wood duck nesting boxes then and the results showed every time I walked the creeks around our rural home with my shotgun and dog. Even as a kid, I appreciated the beauty of the drakes' spectacular plumage, and from time to time I talked about saving one for the taxidermist. But their abundance eventually made even those spectacular little waterfowl seem commonplace, and when my family moved west, the only wood ducks I took with me inhabited my memories.

Subsequent decades spent hunting Montana and Alaska eventually made me appreciate the opportunities I'd missed. Wood ducks are *rara aves* in both locations. By the time I decided I really did want one on the mantle to remind me regularly of nature's capacity for beauty I couldn't find one, at least not during waterfowl season. The one time a lone drake buzzed my spread on a pothole in eastern Montana, the sudden sight of all that flash and color rattled me so badly that I missed. Whenever I thought of the countless woodies I'd plucked in the dark without a second thought years earlier, I remembered the old injunction against casting pearls before swine. And in this scenario of regret, I got to play the pig.

Hence my elation when Rocky arrived back at the blind with a perfect specimen cradled gently in his mouth. Every feather lay neatly in place. Determined to honor the quarry this time around, I broke my shotgun and invited my father to guard the decoy spread while I took time out to reacquaint myself with an old friend.

As it turns out, there are eleven distinct zones of color on a drake wood duck's head from nape to bill tip: four white, two black, two orange, two green, one tan and one purple. Even by the vivid standards of tropical bird life, that's a remarkable degree of visual complexity to pack into a few square inches. An amateur naturalist might wonder: why bother? Practical explanations for this sort of thing almost always involve nothing more romantic than the propagation of the species, but I wasn't buying it. That morning, the little bundle of feathers lying in my hand evoked nothing short of nature's infinite capacity to astound.

With nearly ceremonial care, I wrapped the bird in my stocking cap, leaving my head open to the chill as if to atone for past disrespect to the species. This one was going to the taxidermist. As I finished, my father rose and killed another mallard, reminding me how much I'd enjoyed the company and the pace of the shooting even before the wood duck's arrival. Since there's no law against feeling sentimental while holding a shotgun, I chambered a pair of shells while Rocky completed the retrieve and then accepted my father's invitation to take the next bird that appeared. But when another single burst out of the mist fifteen minutes later, I rose, hesitated and held my fire.

It was another wood duck, and that morning one was enough.

A hen mallard hovers over the decoy spread.

CHAPTER TWO

The Language of Wings

BARELY VISIBLE against the icy gray sky, the first two flights of the morning couldn't have cared less about the hours of dark and lonely labor we'd invested in our spread. As soon as they rose from the distant river, the birds circled for altitude and headed off toward fields of their own choosing as if our decoys hadn't been there, leaving nothing but the reedy echo of goose music behind as they passed. The certainty of the snub felt even more disappointing than the silence of our guns, for the determined vector of their flight and the steady monotony of their wing beats immediately conveyed the futility of our situation. Despite the determination of our calling we never stood a chance of turning either flock, and our hopelessness only made the prairie wind feel colder.

The third flock appeared no lower at first glance, and its flight path seemed programmed to carry it by out of range just like the first two. But even with hundreds of yards of frozen dirt between us, a subtle cue projected a different outcome for this encounter. The lead bird simply skipped a wing beat, creating a momentary syncopation in the rhythm of its flight that rippled backward through the flock one goose at a time. "They're coming in!" I whispered unnecessarily, for my hunting partners had seen just what I had seen and both had been around long enough to appreciate its significance. By the time we'd hissed the dogs into submission on the ground, the birds had begun a slow, stately descent, and the measured pace of their approach erased all memory of the frustration we'd experienced earlier. When we finally rose to shoot, I found myself thinking less about the riot of geese flaring overhead than the subtle cue that announced the end of our long morning's wait: a simple but sufficient moment of hesitation, another figure of speech in the rich language of wings.

The English word pen, like its French and Spanish counterparts, derives from the Latin penna, or feather. While ages spent writing with quill and ink explain this apparent coincidence, language in this case offers a splendid accidental metaphor. Observant hunters care about what they see and hear just as much as they care about what they shoot, and whenever I spend a morning in a blind I find it easy to imagine a special vocabulary written in the language of the wings overhead.

Avian wings feature prominently in numerous cultural traditions, from the Asian fascination with cranes to imitations of the frigate bird in South Pacific island dance rituals. Among modern outdoor enthusiasts, few enjoy better opportunities to appreciate these impressions than the waterfowler. To the upland hunter, wings seldom offer more than buzzes and blurs. Duck and goose hunting, on the other hand, provides a precise, even leisurely, opportunity to see and hear what wings are all about. Consider the duck blind a front row seat at a special performance, and occasional misbehavior on the dog's part (or misses on your own) won't seem nearly so distressing.

Aviation physics explains most of what wings actually do when ducks approach a blind. Lowering flaps increases lift and drag whether the airfoil belongs to a mallard or a 747. This results in lower airspeed and a lower stalling speed, which is just what the pilot needs whether the goal is to land a Super Cub on a gravel bar or settle gently into a decoy spread. While almost all birds employ such techniques in flight, few do so as gracefully and deliberately as waterfowl.

Functionally, a duck's ability to exert such precise control over airfoil characteristics translates into a remarkable combination of speed and agility in the air, especially when it comes to covering vertical distances in a hurry. But there are esthetic implications as well. I know few anatomical parts in nature as expressive as a duck's wing, which can convey attitude and intention at once, at least to those who've bothered to learn the language. I think it's the expressive quality of their wings that makes waterfowl such compelling subjects of visual representation, for no avian family receives more attention from artists and photographers. And ducks and geese always look best in flight, where the language of their wings enjoys its finest opportunity to tell its story.

Of course, this language appeals to the ears as well as the eyes, just as spoken poetry compliments the written word. Someday I'd like to pack a cardiac monitor off to a blind just to see what happens to everyone's pulse rate when the fabric-ripping sound of setting wings first splits the still morning air. That response represents communication, the prime function of any language.

In this case, the language of wings.

Blue-winged teal.

CHAPTER THREE

Opening Day
Blues

THE MARSH LAY QUIETLY before dawn's advance, as if all had forgotten their invitations to the party. The skies remained stubbornly empty as the distant horizon bowed slowly toward the sun, and even the season's last remaining redwings seemed slow to arouse. With stars still visible high overhead and the water's surface calm enough to hold their faint reflection, conditions seemed less than promising for a duck hunt. But it was opening day, and I couldn't imagine anywhere I'd rather be.

Our blind stood in a vast sea of cattails that had risen to exceptional height that year courtesy of generous rainfall on the prairie. When the first flock of blue-wings finally appeared they arrived without warning, skimming in over the top of the reeds at high speed, twisting and turning crazily in the early morning light. As the little wave of birds broke over our decoys, I threw my up gun and snapped off a shot at a teal hurtling past my end of the blind while my hunting partner did the same from his. Neither of us had time to worry about our second barrel. No birds lay before us in the silence that followed, and the dogs (his Chessie, my Lab) offered nothing but contemptuous looks. Why, both dogs seemed to ask, couldn't we have been picked from our litters by people who know how to shoot?

"Looks like you missed," Dick observed as he snapped his double open to reload.

"Looks like you did too," I pointed out as I followed suit.

Ah, blue-wings: has humility ever arrived in a smaller package?

Ask a cross-section of waterfowlers to name their favorite duck and you'll probably hear a lot about mallards, some determined lobbying by pintail enthusiasts, and a few sentimental votes for canvasbacks. But I might well name the diminutive blue-wing teal, an admittedly eccentric choice that warrants explanation.

I've always regarded blue-wings as one of the most beautiful waterfowl in North America. But to appreciate their appearance, one really needs to observe them on the water. Somehow, the drake's delicate mottling and distinctive facial markings seem to disappear on the wing, probably because I'm too busy trying to track that erratic flight path with my gun barrel to notice the nuances of plumage.

Like much of nature's best, blue-wings derive no small measure of their appeal from their evanescent presence. Blue-wings are among the first waterfowl to depart local marshes every year, and up north where I live early season teal hunting usually represents feast or famine. Some opening days I don't see any, and even when they cloud the skies I know they won't last long. Fickle behavior like that makes thoughtful observers appreciate abundance when they can.

For those who love to eat ducks as much as they love to shoot them, there's nothing comparable to a plump blue-wing. I don't know why one species of puddle duck should taste more succulent than all the rest, but blue-wings manage to consistently. Because of their high fat content, I never freeze them, not that any ever last long enough to freeze around our house.

But nothing defines the blue-wing's distinction from the crowd like a flock airborne over a decoy spread. From a technical standpoint, there's a certain consistency to shooting flaring mallards, or even sea ducks skimming along over the waves. But the adjective consistent does not belong to the blue-wing's vocabulary. Utterly unpredictable in flight, they have offered me more crazy shot angles and left me staring stupidly more often than any other waterfowl I know. Although never a competitive shooter, I've always considered myself a competent wing shot, thanks to a fortuitous combination of nature and nurture: parents who produced me capable of pointing where I look and introduced me to the shotgun at an age when most kids are still worrying about toss and catch. But every time hubris rears its ugly head and leaves me thinking I've got it all figured out, teal invariably arrive just in time to set me straight.

As they did that morning in the marsh long ago... For a solid hour, blue-wings came and went, and the number that departed didn't seem to differ much from the number that arrived. Not that we didn't try. In fact, we missed teal in just about every way imaginable as birds zipped and skidded past us at ranges better measured in feet than yards. By mid-morning, we'd finally managed to kill enough to appease the dogs and provide a duck dinner, at least in a low calorie version. The way I saw things, I came, I saw, and even though I didn't conquer, two out of three wasn't all that bad.

Thanks, blue-wings. I needed that.

Hooded merganser.

CHAPTER FOUR

Sawbills

ALTHOUGH THE FOLIAGE along the banks still stood dressed in scarlet and gold, the low autumn sky overhead lay heavy with the promise of winter. The canoe's thin aluminum skin provided little protection from the chill of the water beneath as I sat cross-legged on the bottom, but I was too young to care. As we slid along the creek's dark surface, the rhythmic sound of my father's slowly cadenced paddle strokes rose from the stern while my mother sat motionless in the bow with the shotgun cradled in her arms, much as she'd once cradled me. That was how we hunted ducks back then: floating the local creeks for woodies and whatever else came long, no frills, no fuss, no worries. Even after all these years, I'm not sure I've ever had it better.

Suddenly I felt the stern paddle hesitate. Although I'd been watching the creek ahead as carefully as possible given my mother's presence in my forward line of sight, I hadn't seen a thing. But my father was hunting with his ears as well as his eyes, and moments later I heard the whistle of wings that had sent him into stealth mode. Then the bird rounded the bend in front of us, winging its way upstream in our direction, its white breast flashing in the dull light as it flared too late. I thought I heard my father start to speak, but the shotgun's report drowned his words and then the bird tumbled from the sky and collided with the water beside us.

"What is it?" I wondered aloud as my mother broke the gun open and my father closed the distance to the fallen bird with a few deft paddle strokes. I'd never seen a duck so large or imposing.

"Merganser," my father replied as he rekindled his pipe. As I reached over the gunwale and lifted the floating form into the canoe, I thought my mother had just shot the grandest duck I'd ever seen.

While mergansers--American, red-headed, and hooded--have all received their due on duck stamps, they remain outcasts throughout most of the waterfowling world. Despite their size and striking physical appearance they just don't get much respect, for reasons both complex and arbitrary. Designed for speed in the water rather than the air, they lack their dabbling cousins' grace on the wing. Long and toothy, their bills suggest uncomfortable predatory instincts. And thanks to their carnivorous diet, mergansers can politely be described as challenging in the kitchen and on the table, while realists call them worse.

Back in my student days, I coached a novice friend through the rudiments of duck hunting and sent him off to a local marsh with my shotgun one day when my own schedule made it impossible for me to accompany him. He arrived back at our house late that afternoon looking tired and muddy, but wearing the beaming expression of a young man who has just enjoyed his first successful duck hunt. I could only hope I disguised my sinking spirits when he proudly displayed his bag: a brace of mergansers. To make matters worse, he'd already invited our girlfriends over and promised them a memorable duck dinner. I have no doubt that we provided one.

Over the years, I've learned enough tricks in the kitchen to make mergansers palatable in a pinch, but I still rarely kill them in anything other than subsistence circumstances. After enough nights of rice and beans on wilderness float trips when the moose, caribou, and fish we planned on for dinner have refused to cooperate, just about anything can taste good scorched over an open fire. In the case of mergansers, it helps if you're talking about a lot of nights of rice and beans.

My only deliberate merganser hunts took place when I lived in Alaska. To understand their circumstances, one must appreciate the desperation that creeps into the outdoorsman's heart as long arctic nights tighten their grip on the country and the soul each winter. With the puddle ducks long gone, I'd trudge out to the mouth of the river and pass shoot a merganser or two on the incoming tide just to feel the shotgun thump against my shoulder and watch the dog plunge eagerly into the current. Eating what I shot encouraged the development of my culinary imagination. More important, shooting what I ate contributed to the mental reserves needed to get through another Alaska winter.

I thanked the birds for both, and on the good days they still looked like the grandest ducks I'd ever seen.

Don and Michael: divers on the Columbia.

CHAPTER FIVE

The Case of the Missing Duck

HE WAS A ROGUE AND A FLAWED GENIUS, but John James Audubon's lifework remains a classic among enthusiasts of art and natural history alike. Never equaled in scope or breadth of imagination by any work of its kind, his *Birds of America* changed forever our perception of the New World's natural bounty. Whatever one's views of their artistic merit (and I remain an unabashed admirer), Audubon's prints provide modern American naturalists and outdoorsmen a unique catalog of our avian wildlife.

From the hunter's perspective, the absences from this encyclopedic collection prove illustrative, for the ring-necked pheasant, Hungarian partridge, and chukar, all modern autumn staples, had yet to arrive on our shores. Perhaps more notable is the record of species that have disappeared over the last century, including the passenger pigeon, Carolina parakeet and – until its recent, dramatic, and still controversial rediscovery in an Arkansas swamp – the ivory-billed woodpecker.

But while each of those vanished species is generally better known, the first of Audubon's subjects to disappear completely was a waterfowl last reliably reported from the wild in 1875. Plate #307 in *Birds of America* portrays--in the artist's distinctive, disembodied style-

-a *pas de deux* between a strikingly marked drake and a disinterested hen identified as pied ducks. Subsequent ornithological literature accords *Camptorhynchus labradorius* the common name Labrador duck in recognition of the species' presumptive breeding ground. Such taxonomic confusion is hardly remarkable, since a number of Audubon's birds are identified by names unfamiliar today. Contemporary records suggest that goldeneyes and scoters were also called "pied ducks" once, so the term Labrador duck seems an appropriate way to avoid further confusion despite a lack of objective evidence that the bird spent any time there.

Audubon's own notes acknowledge that he never encountered the species in the wild (his paintings were modeled on preserved specimens collected by friends.) However, his portrayal matches other historical descriptions of a scoter-sized sea duck with, in the male, a dark body, white head, and black longitudinal crown stripe and neck ring. The bird's most distinctive anatomic feature was the membranous enlargement at the end of the bill. During the winter in the mid-1800's, the Labrador duck appeared in east coast game markets where its table quality earned mixed reviews. No one really seems to know where the bird spent its summer breeding season; Labrador seems as good a guess as any.

A century-plus after its disappearance, the obvious question remains: What happened to the Labrador duck? Over-harvest by human predators remains a stock answer, but I have my doubts. While the demise of the passenger pigeon was blamed on hunters for years, one sophisticated analysis showed that even if gunners killed a bird with every shot (yeah, right) America didn't produce enough lead to account for all the pigeons reported in the most reliable estimates of their peak population. Today, most authorities feel that the passenger pigeon succumbed to the destruction of hardwood nesting habitat rather than shotguns.

Granted, the Labrador duck was at least a seasonal market species, but waterfowl that offered more highly esteemed table fare survived market-hunting pressure for decades before the advent of the modern conservation movement. Plume hunters also killed Labrador ducks for the millinery trade, but not in remarkable numbers. On the other hand, the fact that the Labrador duck vanished suddenly during a period of increased human development along the Atlantic coast hardly sounds like a coincidence.

I suspect that the crucial clue lies in the unique appearance of the species' bill, which suggests highly specialized dietary requirements and feeding habits. By accident, humans likely did something--and we'll never know what--to disrupt the bird's food supply. Whatever happened, the time pace of the disaster bears note, for within the course of little more than a decade the Labrador duck went from a market staple to a memory.

In ecological terms, the lessons regarding the need for habitat preservation and environmental vigilance are too obvious to repeat. But as a writer, the exercise of imagination remains part of my job description even when the subject has been gone for a century. My friend Ron Rohrbaugh, a Cornell ornithologist who kindly helped provide background information for this chapter, was directly involved in the recent (and as yet unconfirmed) rediscovery of the "extinct" ivory bill. His sense of excitement proved both inspirational and contagious, and so I have to wonder…

What if some blustery day next season a hunter, crouched down in the rocks on some lonely shore in the North Atlantic, studying a line of bobbing decoys, and listening to his retriever shiver beside him in the blind, spots an unfamiliar black and white duck skimming low across the water…

Barrow's goldeneye.

CHAPTER SIX

Whistlers

ONE GLOOMY MORNING long ago when waterfowl seemed even more mysterious to me than they do today, I stood in a blind beside a Columbia Basin pothole watching my father work Bits, our old short-hair, on a long retrieve a hundred yards away. The air lay perfectly still that morning, and a dense fog bank had rolled in from the river, lowering the ceiling to shotgun range. Suddenly, a perfectly cadenced series of high-pitched whistling sounds rose from the murk overhead. While I didn't know quite what was coming, my instincts prepared me to shoot.

Thanks to some splendid acoustics beneath the fog layer, the sound just kept rising in volume as its source approached, and my pulse rate rose right along with it. When a lone shape finally appeared through the gloom, I had a column of #6's waiting (lead shot, no less; it was that long ago.) The shotgun's report extinguished the whistling, and when the bird hit the water in the middle of the decoys, the sound of the splash seemed to echo forever from the banks of the lonely little pond.

I had to wait for my father to return with the dog to claim my prize. The bundle of sharply contrasting black and white feathers Bits eventually delivered looked utterly alien, since we were new to the West and divers seldom appeared on the inland creeks and ponds I'd hunted in upstate New York. After basking briefly in my father's praise for my shooting, I asked the obvious question: What is it?

"Why, it's a whistler!" he replied with the subtle grin that always preceded paternal lectures in natural history. "You should have been able to figure that out just by listening."

Point taken. But even though I was young in years and short on experience, I knew my bird book, and I didn't remember anything by that name in Petersen's.

"That's the old-time gunners' name for goldeneyes," he explained in response to my perplexed look. "Do you know what they called scaup?"

I didn't, but as we took up our positions in the blind once again, he told me. We talked about unusual common names for waterfowl until a flock of teal arrived to interrupt, and in the shooting that followed I managed to forget most what he told me.

But I never forgot the whistler.

According to recent Fish and Wildlife Service census data, the most abundant duck in North America isn't the familiar mallard, or any of the other dabblers that attract our attention every fall. It's the goldeneye, and in terms of sheer numbers this species leads the pack by a substantial margin.

While goldeneyes enjoy a wide distribution across the continent, they do best on or near big water, fresh or salt. Most of my own experience with whistlers has come in Washington and Alaska, usually near the sea. Here in Montana's Central flyway, their occasional appearance on creeks and rivers late in the season almost always heralds the arrival of bitter weather from the north. While the logical response to this kind of omen, which is usually more accurate than anything professional forecasters have to offer, might be to hunker down in front of the fire, I often choose to go hunting instead, even if that means an extra layer of wool.

Two species of whistlers inhabit North America: the aptly named common goldeneye described above and the less frequently encountered Barrow's. The two can be difficult to tell apart (in fact, the hens are nearly impossible.) In flight, the Barrow's drake shows more black on the wing, and at rest its glossy head looks purple in contrast to the common's green, but absent bright sunlight this field mark is difficult to appreciate. The most reliable difference lies in the shape of the white cheek patch (round in the common, a distinct crescent in the Barrow's), another difficult call when viewed down a ventilated rib in foul weather.

Most of which shouldn't matter much under ordinary circumstances, except that the Barrow's goldeneye holds a special place in my heart. More northern in distribution and even fonder of the sea than their cousins, Barrow's goldeneyes always evoke memories of coastal Alaska, where I've enjoyed them frequently with binoculars and shotgun alike. And what memories those turn out to be: brave dogs in big water, beach landings in Super Cubs, brown bear tracks in the sand. Those who instinctively equate good waterfowling with adventurous waterfowling will understand.

But no matter which species or what venue, the sound of a whistler's wings overhead always makes me stop and think ... about wild ducks and wild places, and a long-ago morning when a kid enjoyed an opportunity to listen to a little more wisdom than he probably deserved to hear.

Mixed bag: woodies and green-wings.

CHAPTER SEVEN

Mixed Bag

THE CEILING COVERED THE SEA like a cold, wet blanket, obscuring the snow-clad peaks rising to the south. Stiff wind pushed against a strong outgoing tide, whipping the bay to an angry froth. Just another fine fall day on Kodiak, the kind no one loves like a duck hunter.

The last to leave the skiff, I heard a shotgun bark as I crossed the isthmus at the mouth of the lagoon, and by the time I reached my friends they were arguing over the identity of the duck one of them had just shot. He had originally pegged the bird as a harlequin hen, but eventually recognized it as something different. "Female ring-necked duck," I replied with a bit more confidence than I really felt. None of us had ever seen one in that area. When I eventually confirmed my call with the help of a well-thumbed bird book, the satisfaction felt as rewarding as the smoothest double of the day.

I've always regarded variety as an essential element of the duck hunting experience. Dozens of waterfowl species ply the continent's four major flyways. Appreciating the differences among them and being able to identify them accurately can become a gratifying outdoor skill in its own right. Granted, I know veteran duck hunters who would be happy to spend the rest of their careers shooting nothing but drake mallards, but I think they're overlooking an important part of the show.

Everyday fare in one location can arouse a rare sense of delight in another. Consider the case of the wood ducks described earlier. When I was a kid back East, they made up the majority of our bag and we regarded them as commonplace. Since moving west 40 years ago, the occasional woodie I've killed in the Pacific and Central Flyways inevitably felt like a special gift.

For hunters accustomed to a steady menu of dabblers in the heartland, a sea duck expedition can arouse a true sense of the exotic. Harlequins! Scoters! Eiders! Between the challenge of sorting out new species and the unique flavor of the maritime environment, even veterans often experience a child-like sense of excitement.

From a practical standpoint, field identification isn't nearly as complicated as it seems. Legal considerations are always paramount. Fortunately, staying on the right side of the law usually boils down to learning a few easy species with restricted limits. Where I live, that means being able to identify pintails, redheads, canvasbacks, scaup and hooded mergansers, all of which are obvious. Granted, distinguishing a female common goldeneye from a female Barrow's over decoys forty yards away can be impossible, but no regulation requires that you do so.

Experienced hunters eventually develop their own methods of making accurate calls in the field. No wonder; we have to identify our subjects on the wing, in low light, without benefit of binoculars. Wing-beat pattern, flight characteristics, and silhouette accurately narrow the possibilities even at a distance. Final identification often depends upon cues seldom stressed in standard field guides. Around my home, the most important practical distinction lies between hen and drake mallards. Years ago, I learned to forget about looking for green heads except in bright sunlight. Instead, I concentrate on picking out the sharp demarcation between the light belly and dark thorax on the drakes as they pass overhead, a simple trick that leads to few mistakes. But they do occur, and while the law allows two hens, I pack up after the first as a form of penance.

The late season is winding down on the high plains now, and I haven't seen anything but mallards in the valley for weeks. In fact, three drakes lie at our feet in the snow, a gift from the first flock to visit the decoys. They're all prime birds: plump, hefty, and crimson-legged, with triple curls in their tail feathers. But I feel hungry for something else. Not something better, just something different.

Suddenly a series of rhythmic, high-pitched whistles rises through the crisp air, announcing a wish about to be granted. "Goldeneye!" I hiss to Lori even before the bird rounds the bend downstream. As starkly black and white as the winter landscape, the lone drake couldn't care less about our decoys, but his route up the creek carries him by within range and moments later the dog is surging through the current toward the fall.

With a potential limit of mallards still ahead, some hunters might have ignored that bird. But its white cheek patch and dramatic markings suddenly unleash a flood of memories, of bays and ponds and rivers I haven't seen in years. Variety really is the spice of life, and I'll take mine as spicy as possible.

Don and Kenai with an early season greenhead.

CHAPTER EIGHT

The All-American Duck

MY EARS ANNOUNCED the birds' arrival as the sunrise broke slowly across the lonely prairie to the east: a rich, soothing chorus of chuckles followed by a quick crescendo of air tearing through cupped primaries. Nestled beside me in the coffin blind, Rocky began to quiver as I scanned the awakening sky. It took me a moment or two to locate the flock in the first minutes of legal shooting light, but I'd already made the ID on the basis of sound alone. Our first visitors that morning were mallards.

We'd set up for geese in a windswept stubble field, and with an hour of pre-dawn labor invested in our vast spread of shells, discretion might have made us hold our fire and wait for bigger game yet to come. But some offerings prove too tempting to resist. "What do you think?" I heard Jeff Lander whisper as the flock turned upwind and committed to land. "Let's do it!" I replied without hesitation, and we did.

I've always found shooting from a supine position awkward and my second barrel punished me as I crumpled a drake flaring overhead. But by then the sky was raining mallards, the dogs were happy, and so were we. I'll never know whether that impulsive decision cost us any geese that morning, but I'll never care either. Nature sometimes offers gifts that would be impolitic to refuse, none more so than a brace of grain-stuffed northern greenheads.

Mom, apple pie... mallards. There's something quintessentially American about *Anas platyrhynchos* (although, like many of "our" waterfowl, they enjoy wide geographic distribution as a result of human introductions, and I've run into them in locations as diverse as Australia and southern Africa). Ask a roomful of kids to name one wild duck and the mallard will top the list every time. And their popularity among hunters is such that some experienced hands shoot them exclusively and regard all other species as little more than distractions.

There are objective grounds for the esteem mallards enjoy within the waterfowling community. They are our largest puddle duck, and a single prime late season specimen will feed a hungry hunter in style. They often travel in large flocks that provide an unparalleled spectacle over decoy spreads. And while one can make arguments for the superiority of pintails, blue-wings, or canvasbacks on the table, mallards are perhaps the most consistent of all. Anyone who can cook a duck can cook a mallard.

But since other ducks are fun to shoot and gratifying to eat, the mallard's universal popularity must depend on certain intangibles, prime among them familiarity. The drake's glossy, emerald green head provides an unmistakable field mark that distinguishes it from various drab-colored dabblers that novices often find confusing. This principle, rather than concern over reproductive biology, may explain the short shrift accorded mallard hens, which tend to blend in with the females of a half dozen other puddle duck species in the popular imagination.

In the end, returning from the field with a limit of greenheads hanging from a game strap represents a singular accomplishment. The weight alone, unmatched by a limit of any other puddle duck species, suggests a successful hunt for big game. Those glossy heads and chestnut breast feathers demand the eye's attention just as they confirm the successful distinction of drakes from hens on the hunter's part. No matter where the hunt takes place, the whole experience feels positively… well, American. Just like Mom and apple pie.

During the late season here on the high plains, mallards account for such a high percentage of the waterfowl bag that the occasional appearance of a green-wing or goldeneye inevitably arouses excitement in the blind, because it offers the opportunity for a "free" duck (due to the Central Flyway limit structure), and a steady diet of anything evokes a longing for variety. This phenomenon explains my excitement over other, less highly regarded species when I travel elsewhere to hunt with friends, most of whom cannot understand why I would actually pass up a shot at a mallard.

But this morning it's been another all-mallard affair, and three of the flyway's finest already lie behind Rocky on the snow. It's just the two of us today, but I feel no regrets. As much as I enjoy good human company in the blind, I know the dog can be relied upon to laugh at my jokes and turn his head discreetly in the event of an embarrassing miss. And suddenly here they come: a dozen hefty northern birds that seem determined to provide me with just such an opportunity.

As someone once observed, don't throw me in that briar patch. These are All-American ducks, and I stand ready to do my duty as a citizen.

Lori and Rocky with an Alberta speck.

CHAPTER NINE

Speck-tacular

FOR ONCE, our timing seemed impeccable. A cold snap high in the Canadian interior had pushed birds down in waves, and as we labored through the pre-dawn darkness we'd heard the goose talk from the distant reservoir build relentlessly. With our vast decoy spread complete at last, we surveyed our handiwork with satisfaction, convened for an unnecessary last minute pep talk, and dispersed to our coffin blinds to wait and hope.

No birds appeared during the course of the long prairie sunrise, but the combination of hot coffee from the thermos and Rocky's cold muzzle against my cheek kept my eyes wide open despite the emptiness of the skies overhead. Suddenly, the racket from the reservoir reached a crescendo. No one needed to announce that the birds were finally in the air. Hissing at the dog to remind him of his manners, I kept my attention focused upon the fading pink clouds suspended high across the sky to the east, the direction from which the birds would come.

And there they finally were at last: undulating lines of hundreds if not thousands of greater Canadas silhouetted against the sun. The first wave bypassed us to the north, but before I could register disappointment I spotted a dozen birds descending over the edge of our field with their wings set as rigidly as sculpted bronze. Smaller and more delicate in outline than the honkers that had overlooked us earlier, these geese looked alien and unfamiliar at first. But then I remembered what varied possibilities southern Alberta has to offer just as someone cried "Specks!" from an adjacent blind.

"Let's make this count," I whispered to Rocky, and then I began to calculate the timing of my rise.

With the exception of the Aleutian emperor, *Anser albifrons* may be the least familiar of all North American geese despite regionally enthusiastic followings among waterfowlers, who prize them for their elegance on the wing and superiority on the table. Although properly known as greater white fronted geese (to distinguish them from the lesser European version), hunters invariably refer to these small, drably marked geese as speckle-bellies, or just plain specks. With circumpolar breeding distribution and long migration routes that take them as far south as Mexico, they see more of the world than almost any other goose species.

Nonetheless, it's possible to spend a lot of time in North American waterfowl habitat without ever running into them. I encountered my first specks while floating the Missouri River years ago. I lived in a remote corner of the prairie then, and Huck Finn canoe trips down the wild Missouri were part of our regular autumn agenda, with mule deer in the breaks, pheasants on the islands, and a chance at whatever waterfowl happened to be trading along the river. The specks came around the bend in front of us as an unexpected surprise one October afternoon, and I identified them just in time to drop one and give young Sky his first opportunity to retrieve a goose. Upon our eventual return to civilization, such as it was, we cooked the bird and declared the species' reputation on the table completely justified. Ever since, whenever I've faced mixed flocks of geese over decoys I've preferentially shot specks just because I love to eat them.

Living on the cusp between the Central and Pacific flyways now, I hardly ever see specks in my home county, and I've never had an opportunity to hunt them where those long flights converge for the winter farther south. But southern Canada doesn't lie all that far away, and I'm lucky enough to have friends there who share my passion for waterfowl. Six-hour drives north across the continent's prairie heartland have become a part of my autumn schedule just as Missouri River float trips once were. Of course I can shoot ducks and geese closer to home, but it's always good to see old friends... especially when the reunion includes an opportunity to hunt my favorite geese.

Few moments in the outdoors demand attention like geese inbound to a spread of decoys: the graceful arc of their wings' leading edges viewed head on, the last subdued vocalizations as they extend their gear and prepare to land. Sometimes that long final approach seems to last forever, and as often as not I wish it would.

But 40 yards out, one wise old bird smelled a rat. Suddenly, geese were clawing their way back into the sky as we threw open the tops of our blinds and tried to isolate targets from the flock. Confused by the fog of war, our coordination faltered and we doubled up on a bird or two before we settled down with what shells remained. Finally, it was Rocky's turn.

Speck-tacular.

Marshall Davidson's Glory with a hen shoveler.

CHAPTER TEN

No Ugly Ducklings

A FEW HOURS INTO A RECENT HUNT along the Gulf Coast with our old Texas friends Dick Negley and Marshall Davidson, I'd observed more varieties of ducks than I'd seen all season back on the high plains. Wind had pushed big flocks of divers inland from San Antonio Bay, and canvasbacks had been screaming by all morning. Scaup and occasional redheads rounded out the diver contingent. I'd led off the morning with a drake gadwall, and we'd subsequently added both blue-wings and green-wings to the bag.

This great avian hodge-podge was of practical as well as biological interest. A conservative five duck limit was in effect, restricted further to one canvasback, one pintail, or one mallard hen. With so many birds in the air that morning, I largely felt content to observe while I tried to decide between a drake pintail or canvasback as my one high-end duck for the day. Besides, the snow geese were due back from the fields at any time, and I knew our morning wouldn't suffer from lack of shooting opportunities.

Suddenly, a high single appeared straight out in front of us with its wings set. The frontal angle eliminated the bird's profile, making precise identification difficult. A flash of white in its plumage suggested the bird might be a pintail drake. But as it turned to glide past the outer perimeter of the decoy spread, I finally saw a clear silhouette against the backlight reflecting from the pond's surface, a definitive visual cue that might as well have been a neon sign. Impulsively, I rose and killed the first shoveler I'd shot in years.

Glory, Marshall's female black Lab, made short work of the retrieve. As soon as she delivered the bird to hand I felt my attention drawn inexorably toward the defining feature of the species: its impossibly exaggerated, spatulate bill. On the wing the bird had looked delicate and graceful, flying much like the teal to which it's closely related; now it seemed almost grotesque. Since we were obviously going to enjoy ample opportunity to shoot ducks that day, I sat down in the blind without bothering to reload and thought about shovelers and the arbitrary definitions of beauty we bring with us to the field.

Until recently, *Anas clypeata* was officially known as the northern shoveler. That leading adjective suggests the existence of other shoveler species outside North America, as is indeed the case. During my wide travels afield I've encountered the Cape shoveler in South Africa and the Australasian shoveler in Queensland. Oddly enough, our own "northern" shoveler occasionally appears in both locations as well. No matter what the object of study, worldwide distribution and the existence of multiple closely related species are two reliable indicators of biological success, attesting to adaptability, dominance of an important ecological niche, or both. No matter what we may think of its looks, the shoveler must be doing something right.

As members of the function-is-beauty school of thought should have no trouble appreciating... No matter how improbable the species' bill may strike the casual observer esthetically, it's a marvel of adaptive design that allows the bird to filter high volumes of pond water while the fine projections inside trap tiny particles of food much like a whale's baleen. This catchall filter feeding capability explains the shoveler's omnivorous diet, which typically includes a wide variety of invertebrates as well as the dabblers' usual vegetarian fare. Bottom-of-the-pond feeding habits may contribute to the shoveler's shaky reputation as human table fare (which I find exaggerated), but they also explain its ability to thrive when more selective feeders are suffering through a lean year. No matter how ugly we might find that bill, it allows the shoveler to laugh all the way to the next breeding season. In biological terms, that's all that counts.

Practical considerations aside, it's remarkable how the appearance of the shoveler's highly adapted bill dominates its appearance, like a wart on the end of an otherwise gorgeous princess's nose. Otherwise, a hen shoveler looks dull and drab much like other female puddle ducks, for just the same reason: mottled brown feathers confer the ability to hide from predators while sitting on a nest. But a drake shoveler in breeding plumage is one of the most visually striking waterfowl in North America, with powder blue wing patches, rufous sides that contrast dramatically against the white breast, and a golden eye that glows distinctively from the emerald face. Why can't we get around that oddly shaped bill long enough to appreciate all this?

It's not as if distinctive, highly adapted bills are incompatible with conventional notions of avian beauty. From curlews to hummingbirds, examples abound. Consider the case of the canvasback, whose sloping facial profile is nearly as distinctive as the shoveler's. Yet many experienced hands, myself included, consider a drake canvasback one of the most attractive waterfowl on the continent even as they pass up one shoveler after another because they don't want to be seen shooting a "spoonbill". Go figure.

Out in the Texas marsh that day, I'd devoted several minutes of potential shooting time to this analysis when Glory's ears perked up and the sound of setting wings tore through the air. The new arrival over the decoys was a lone drake pintail. Although I never set out to be an art collector, I've picked up a number of First of Nation prints at various Ducks Unlimited banquets. A remarkable number of them feature pintails; there isn't a shoveler in the lot. The sprig that my wife Lori was about to kill looked undeniably beautiful. Was it really more beautiful than a shoveler?

Perhaps it's best to remember that all waterfowl look the way they do for the same basic reason: that's what works for them. According to that analysis, there are no ugly ducklings.

Drake gadwall on the wing.

CHAPTER ELEVEN

Field Marks

IN OUR CORNER of the Central Flyway, the vast majority of ducks taken after Thanksgiving are mallards. True to form, all five birds lying beside us in the snow that morning had green heads. But thanks to the specifics of the legal limit ("... six ducks, no more than five of which may be mallards...") , the ability to identify birds on the wing rapidly and accurately yields a practical dividend: an occasional opportunity to shoot one extra duck. As soon as I saw the next single set it's wings and head for the decoys, I urged Lori to stand and take the shot.

"It's a hen!" she protested.

"No it isn't!" I replied, and since the bird wasn't going to circle the spread indefinitely while we debated, I did the ungentlemanly thing and killed it myself. "It's a drake gadwall," I explained as Rocky hit the water. "Very unusual to see one here this late." Moments later, I was pointing out the dark stern and white wing specula as we dodged water flying from the dog.

"I can see the difference now," Lori said. "But up in the sky it looked like a hen mallard. How did you know it was a gadwall?"

"Because it looked like a gadwall," I replied. Sorry, but that was the best explanation I could muster.

Some of us may have been born with silver spoons in our mouths, but I had to settle for feathers. Birds fascinated me as soon as I was old enough to walk, and I was reading Roger Tory Petersen when other kids were sounding out See Spot Run. Other arguably more definitive American bird books have appeared in the decades since, but my own sense of bird life has always been grounded in the Field Guides.

An accomplished artist as well as a naturalist, Peterson was astute enough to recognize that for purposes of identification schematic illustrations are more helpful than stark realism as captured by a camera's lens. As he himself put it: "A drawing can often do more than a photograph to emphasize field marks. A photograph is the record of a fleeting instant; a drawing is a composite of an artist's experience." Like countless other amateur ornithologists of my generation, I grew up with Peterson's composites indelibly imprinted in my brain.

And I still find them useful. If you're trying to remember how to tell a lesser scaup from a greater through binoculars, there's no handier reference. The paradoxical point, however, is how little those concise field marks have to do with identifying birds where it counts most: in the duck blind. During prime waterfowling hours, flat light often makes even obvious markings and coloration difficult to appreciate. How often, for example, do drake mallards' heads really appear green at first legal shooting light?

Fortunately, none of this matters much to veteran waterfowl hunters, who don't identify birds on the basis of static images. In fact, the great weakness of all bird books is that they fail to convey a sense of what really counts in the field: how ducks appear in silhouette and how they move. Even in low light, a brief glance at a flock's behavior on the wing should distinguish dabblers from divers and the appropriate algorithms proceed quickly from there. Out west, no puddle duck looks as blocky as a mallard, while a pintail's delicate profile should be apparent in any light. Teal dip and flutter like moths and their flight patterns distinguish them from other ducks even when there's nothing else in the air to provide a size comparison. The unlikely gadwall we spotted from the blind that cold December morning? The narrow profile of its wings established that it wasn't a mallard, but it just didn't maneuver as gracefully as a pintail. At some subliminal level, I had all the rest worked out well before it flew into shotgun range.

The drawback to these perfectly reliable means of distinguishing ducks on the wing is that they can be appreciated by no means other than experience. No bird book in the world can convey a sense of how different varieties of waterfowl fly. Even veterans have trouble articulating how they see what they see and know what they know. Witness my utterly unscientific explanation to Lori in the blind that morning.

In contrast to upland gunners, waterfowlers really need to know their birds. Legal considerations apply, and no matter which flyway's regulations you're hunting under the time will come when you'll have to be able to distinguish one species from another in order to stay on the right side of the law. With all due respect to Peterson, the best place to learn the game is in the field.

Fortunately, that's the only classroom in the world that's never made me long for the bell to ring.

Gulf Coast green-wings.

CHAPTER TWELVE

Green-Wing Mornings

ON THE FIRST DAY of a recent trip to hunt with friends on the Texas Gulf Coast, Lori and I arrived at our blind in the dark after a disorienting airboat ride through fog so thick I could barely tell up from down much less north from south as we ran. After pitching two dozen decoys into the dark, we settled back and used the wait for shooting light to savor the sounds of the tidal marsh awakening all around us, an exotic avian chorus of croaks, whistles, quacks, and screeches that made it hard to believe we hadn't stamped our passports the day before. Above all, it wasn't snowing. When you've left a savage high plains winter behind, who could ask for anything more?

Dawn eventually limped across the horizon like an old man on crutches, with the sun burning ineffectually somewhere beyond the fog. My watch said shooting light, but my eyes told me otherwise. We left our shotguns unloaded for an extra twenty minutes until I felt confident that I could identify ducks accurately in the gloom. By then the unfamiliar birdcalls had turned into avocets, spoonbills, and a host of other wading birds. Our friends were shooting elsewhere about the marsh, and I could safely identify most of the ducks overhead as green-wings. "Let's load up," I said to Lori.

I knew we were in for a challenging morning. Because of the fog we couldn't see the ducks until they were already in range, which left just a brief interval to shoulder a shotgun, swing, and fire before they rocketed back into the mist. Furthermore, the tricky Texas duck limit that year—one pintail or one canvasback or one hen mallard or one mottled duck—made fast, accurate identification mandatory. The solution was obvious: stick to the teal. Fortunately, the green-wings obliged.

I rarely get to enjoy an honest teal shoot at home nowadays. The blue-wings are often gone by opening day, and migrating green-wings just don't frequent our cusp between the Central and Pacific flyways. The first half hour of shooting light that morning reminded me what I'd been missing. We couldn't sit back down on the bench; the little birds appeared and disappeared too quickly. Instead, we stood at port-arms, watched the fog overhead, and cried "Teal!" whenever one of us could make a positive ID. The shooting that followed felt as challenging and rewarding as anything I'd experienced in a duck blind for years.

With room for one bird left in my limit, I settled back to offer some unnecessary shooting advice to Lori and think about taking the next drake pintail that circled our decoy spread. But in the end the lure of a pure teal limit proved too tempting to ignore. We each shot our last green-wing of the day and retired to camp to plan a snow goose hunt that afternoon.

When we rose in the dark the next morning I saw stars gleaming down through a crystal clear sky and donned an extra layer of clothing in anticipation of a chilly morning. But when I stepped outside I found weather more appropriate to a Bahamian bonefish camp than a mid-winter duck hunt and couldn't get my heavy sweater off fast enough. Before we climbed into the airboat, we even had to douse ourselves with bug repellant to keep from being carried off by mosquitoes. The world of waterfowl we'd left behind in Montana—geese on ice-choked rivers, mallards on steaming spring creeks—could have belonged to another planet.

By the time we set the blocks and settled into the blind the mosquitoes had disappeared, thanks to a rapidly freshening breeze from the bay. And it was the wind that defined the shooting as we concentrated again on the abundant green-wings. Excellent visibility made it easy to see the birds coming, but I had almost forgotten how a stiff breeze can make an inbound flock of teal defy the laws of aeronautics. When the first set plummeted from the sky, zoomed across the spread just above the waves, and accelerated back to altitude in perfect formation, I could only stare in admiration. When we finally started shooting, we each missed a couple of birds before we settled down, regained our form, and completed two more limits of green-wings to contribute to the table that night.

When the third morning of the hunt broke clear and still, Lori and I decided to concentrate on photography while we casually shot a final limit of teal... a decision that only proved how easily nature can make the over-confident hunter come a cropper. During the long hour between shooting light for shotguns and shooting light for cameras several tempting pintails visited the spread, but we ignored them. And by the time rich sunlight finally flooded the marsh, I realized we'd been had: the teal were all sitting on the slick water far out in the bay. We stuck it out all morning without firing a shot.

Writers have a habit of searching for meaning in the simplest events, and perhaps there's nothing at stake here save for the realization that shooting in fascinating places accompanied by good friends remains one of life's true pleasures.

But three consecutive mornings spent hunting one variety of duck in the same place led to three entirely different experiences. I think that observation goes a long way toward explaining our collective fascination with waterfowling, an undertaking in which there are never any givens. Nature sees to that. A tennis court is always a tennis court, but a duck marsh is never the same twice and neither are its myriad inhabitants. Every time we rise in the dark and head to the field we face an element of the unknown, no matter how confident we feel that earlier events will repeat themselves. In a world rendered increasingly predictable by technology, we need such comeuppance more and more. That's why wild places matter.

Just like the teal.

Don with a Columbia River can.

CHAPTER THIRTEEN

The King of Ducks

I WAS SITTING beside a prairie pothole in eastern Montana one blustery morning nearly four decades ago when a line of ducks appeared over the far end of the pond traveling in tight formation low to the water. I couldn't identify them at first, but when they turned at the far edge of the decoy spread the lead bird revealed an unmistakable profile, and I reacted in time to drop the drake at the tail end of the flock. My Lab soon completed a long but otherwise routine retrieve and delivered the first canvasback I'd ever held in my hand. That was an expensive shot in the days of the point count limit, since my can shut me down on a morning that might have produced a lot of 10-point blue-wings and pintail drakes. But I wouldn't have missed the opportunity for the world.

Although I practically grew up in a duck blind, I don't remember seeing a single canvasback in upstate New York where my hunting career started. The little beaver ponds we hunted there held their share of woodies, teal, and occasional black ducks, but they weren't big enough to attract divers. Furthermore, there just weren't a lot of cans anywhere when I started hunting ducks. The story of the species' decline and recovery provides a neat synopsis of the history of North American waterfowl conservation, from what went wrong to what finally went right.

Esteemed by sportsmen for its size, striking appearance, and the challenging gunning it provides, the canvasback suffered historically from another asset that became a near-fatal flaw: its table quality. In contrast to most divers the can is a vegetarian, sharing its specific name, *valiseneria*, with the wild celery upon which it preferentially feeds. By the late 1800's canvasbacks had become a high-end restaurant staple, and vintage menus show that it was the only wild duck patrons routinely ordered by name. That made the bird a commodity and created a demand that market hunters were happy to oblige.

In 1897, a market hunter named Forest McNeir went canvasback hunting one morning on the Texas Gulf Coast. "They had to pass our end of the island," he later recalled. "We didn't shoot into the front end of the big bunches as they dived for our decoys, but we tore into the back end, and shot all the scattering ducks that came along… When we quit shooting, all the rushes around our skiff were standing up from the heat of those 300 rounds of black powder. We picked up 192 fat canvasbacks, worth big money in the New York market for the Christmas holidays."

The same menus that confirm the can's original restaurant popularity also document the effect that kind of market pressure inflicted. When they were still plentiful before the turn of the century, a canvasback dinner cost about $20 in modern currency. By 1910, cans were scarce enough to command a $100 price tag.

Sportsmen led the way in the recovery of the continent's waterfowl populations, first by drafting landmark legislation like the Migratory Bird Treaty Act, then by picking up the tab for the enforcement of modern wildlife law through the Pittman-Robertson Act, and finally through habitat work spearheaded by Ducks Unlimited. But by the time the USFWS began to provide a scientific census of North American waterfowl, the can was still in trouble even when other species were thriving again, a realization that led to a season closure on canvasbacks in the 1970's.

What was wrong with the king of ducks? A brief literature search revealed the following theories: poisoning by lead shot, a decline in wild celery due to water pollution, alterations in winter habitat by hurricanes, pesticides, drought, loss of breeding habitat to agriculture, spring egg harvest by Alaska Natives, parasites, increased predatory impact on nesting hens by raccoons, illegal hunting, and degradation of freshwater habitat by invasive carp. Such abundance of hypotheses usually means that no one really knows the answer. Since the problem was relatively specific to canvasbacks, I suspect that their prolonged decline reflects initial reduction in numbers below a critical threshold by intense market hunting coupled with the delay in recovery inherent to any species with relatively rigid habitat requirements.

The can's current population status represents a biological success story to rival the recovery of the wild turkey--with some important qualifications. From a population nadir of less than 300,000 in the 1980's, numbers climbed to 850,000 by 2007, well above the North American Waterfowl Management Plan goal. It was finally time to start hunting the king of ducks again.

I was ready. That first can I banged down on the prairie all those years ago was also my last for several decades, at first by legal necessity and then by virtue of voluntary restraint. But I still couldn't quite bring myself to take advantage of the two-canvasback daily limit in effect in some areas that year. I chose instead to take an occasional bird and regard each one as big game. And every time I sat down at the table to eat one—roasted plain, with no distractions between the duck and my palette—I remembered those gourmet diners forking out $100 a crack for the same privilege.

The following year's season closure simply demonstrated that canvasback populations will require careful monitoring throughout our lifetime. Our ability to enjoy limited hunting for the king of ducks in 2009 came as welcome news. But whether I choose to appreciate them as part of a memorable hunt, a special wild game dinner, or simply a stunning sight through my binoculars, cans always allow the satisfaction of knowing I've been a part—albeit a small one—of something even more important. The fact is that they wouldn't be here today for anyone to enjoy without duck hunters and Ducks Unlimited.

So take a bow… and enjoy your next encounter with the king of ducks.

Rocky, proud of his first mottled duck.

CHAPTER FOURTEEN

The Mottled Duck

THE WEATHER THAT JANUARY MORNING on the Texas Gulf Coast would have done justice to a late season hunt along a steaming spring creek back home in Montana. The sheet of ice that had formed overnight nearly covered the surface of the pond in front of the blind, and I had to stomp out a hole just to hold the decoys. The first hour of shooting light had produced nothing but a single flight of teal, and Lori and I had both fanned as they rocketed past us on the driving north wind. The egrets and ibises gliding by overhead looked dazed and confused in the ice fog, as if they were struggling to awaken from some collective nightmare. I was cold, Lori was cold, and even Rocky, our veteran yellow Lab, looked ready to quit beneath his coat of frozen salt mud... and this was a dog that routinely hunted waterfowl at ten below.

Suddenly I spotted a pair of ducks across the marsh. Although still too far away to identify with certainty, they were clearly larger than teal, and their wing beat pattern did not suggest the pintails or divers that frequent the area. Since mallards are rare there I guessed widgeon or gadwall, but that hypothesis didn't seem quite right either.

The birds turned in response to my first call as if they'd received a command from Air Traffic Control. As the pair sped across the pond in our direction, enough muted sunlight finally reached them to provide a look at their plumage. Two hen mallards? Their coloration looked a bit too dark, evoking vague memories of the black ducks I used to shoot in the Atlantic Flyway back when I was a kid. Then a light began to flash suddenly somewhere in the frozen recesses of my brain.

The connection actually began a week earlier when I dug out the dog-eared Peterson's Field Guide that contains my life list of birds in order to add a couple of new species I'd identified while hunting quail in the Arizona desert. I'm a fairly casual birder—I often observe birds in the field but seldom go afield just to observe birds. The numerous gaps and holes in my life list reflect that lack of dedication with two notable exceptions that shouldn't surprise anyone: upland game birds and waterfowl. In fact, I realized once I'd places checkmarks beside Anna's hummingbird and the ladder-backed woodpecker, I'd not only identified almost all of them—I'd taken representatives of most species with my shotgun. Save for the rare Asian strays that eluded me even when I lived in Alaska, there was only one exception in the puddle duck column: the mottled duck.

My lack of familiarity with *Anas fulvigula* derived purely from geographical considerations. Uniquely adapted to breed in southern marshes, the mottled duck inhabits a restricted range about the Gulf Coast from northern Mexico to Florida (where it exists as a distinct subspecies known locally if incorrectly as the Florida mallard). As a rare example of a non-migratory puddle duck, it never reaches areas I hunt regularly.

Despite my inherent fascination with new species, I felt an odd hesitation about the possibility of taking even the one mottled duck the Texas daily limit allowed. My concern wasn't based on biology. While the species had its ups and downs over the previous decade, its current status didn't proscribe taking one occasionally, and threats to the species' future derive more from habitat degradation by coastal development and hybridization with closely related mallards and black ducks than from appropriately regulated hunting. The problem was my lack of experience with its appearance and both sexes' close resemblance to hen mallards, which I'd spent many seasons training myself to avoid shooting.

Prior to our trip to Texas I had prepared myself for the possibility of a mottled duck encounter by studying the books. I learned that the mottled duck is distinguished from the mallard hen by its darker overall appearance, the sharp demarcation between its light head and dark body, the pure yellow bill, and the absence of white in the flight primaries. But I was still worried; those sounded like subtle differences to recognize in dull light while visually tracking a speeding bird on the wing. And I really hate shooting hen mallards by mistake.

In the event, most of that worry proved unnecessary. I might have felt less confident had we been hunting an area inhabited by black ducks now that I haven't seen one in decades, but a mottled duck doesn't look nearly as similar to a mallard hen as I'd expected. As the pair I'd called in set their wings over the outer edge of the decoy spread, I whispered "Mottled ducks!" and thumbed my safety.

After listening to me go on about this possibility all the way from Montana, Lori courteously kept her seat and let me stand to make or break my first encounter with the species on my own. I was aware of wanting to drop the lead bird more than I'd wanted to kill a duck in some time, and equally aware that such mental gymnastics can often become a prelude to an embarrassing miss. But the bird crumpled at my shotgun's report, and suddenly old Rocky was slogging off through the ice like a dog half his age. Moments later, the bird lay resting gently in my gloved hand.

Many elements of the waterfowling experience involve celebrations of the familiar: a return to a favorite blind, an early morning breakfast with old friends and hunting partners, one more retrieve from an aging dog. But from new puppies to new places, duck hunting also offers nearly infinite ways to test the limits of the envelope these experiences define. And sometimes the challenge of the new can appear in a form as simple as a single, drably colored duck.

Harlequins at spring bear camp.

CHAPTER FIFTEEN

Send in the Clowns

ALTHOUGH WE'D SET UP on a lee shore, surge from nearby Kupreanof Straight, encouraged by a freshening westerly gale, was battering our decoys around mercilessly in the surf. Compounding our problems, the tide was dropping rapidly, which meant that every 20 minutes one of us had to emerge from the shelter of our beach log blind and pitch the blocks out past the breakers all over again. Given the eerie, distant quality of December sunlight on Kodiak Island, it was difficult to tell how much time had passed since daybreak's official arrival. But I did know that I was cold and wet, and that if something didn't happen soon the lure of the woodstove and a hot breakfast back in the cabin would likely prove too much to resist.

But then something did happen, as the whistle of wings rose above the sound of the wind and the waves. The birds were goldeneyes, and Barrow's goldeneyes at that: rare game in my new Montana home but everyday fare along the coast of Alaska. When they roared by at the periphery of shotgun range, hunting partner Ernie Holland and I rose together, sent two drakes tumbling across the waves with our first barrels, and then held our fire as the rest of the flock flared upward into the ominous sky and disappeared.

Our restraint arose out of respect for Yaeger, our friend Bob May's Chessie and our only means of retrieving game that morning. Yaeger was the toughest sea-going duck dog I've ever met, but given the wind and tide we knew that even he would have difficulty keeping track of more than two downed birds at a time. But Yaeger, never enthusiastic about the constraints of formal command, was already crashing through the surf by the time I lowered my shotgun, and five minutes later both birds were resting beside us on a log.

We'd barely settled back down out of the wind by the time another flock rounded the point, but this time I had to strain my eyes against the spray to identify the birds, which were smaller and darker than the goldeneyes. In contrast to the day's first set, this one seemed genuinely interested in our decoys and headed straight toward us like horses returning to a familiar barn. When the lead bird banked hard at the edge of the spread, I felt my pulse quicken as its clownish facial markings registered through the gloom. This was what I had come to Kodiak for this time, and I rose to accept the invitation.

The species' scientific name—*Histrionicus histrionicus*—should tell us something about the way human observers have always regarded the harlequin duck. (Histrionic: adj. 1. of or pertaining to actors or acting.) Indeed, the drake's striking appearance—which my worn copy of Petersen's describes as "bizarre"—seems more likely the product of grease paint than genetics. The bird's common name enforces the impression of playful artifice. Harlequin was a recurring comic character in commedia dell'arte, usually dressed in diamond-patterned tights and carrying a wooden sword (or slapstick), an apt allusion for a duck that looks more comical than any other on the continent.

Indeed, one's first good look at a harlequin duck in the wild is apt to elicit stunned disbelief, especially if binoculars allow the observer to appreciate the drake's rich auburn flanks and the bold, white markings on the face and neck, drawn precisely enough to suggest the work of an artist's stencil.

When faced with such a natural anomaly, the curious student of natural history must wonder what purpose it can serve. Reproductive advantage is always a good guess, and personal observations support this thesis in the case of the harlequin duck. The camp from which I guide bear hunters on the Alaska Peninsula sits near the junction of an inland lake and a famous trout stream. Harlequins gather there in great numbers during the spring season, providing a wonderful opportunity to study their courtship displays. Drake harlequins seem much more aggressive than other male divers, often gathering in groups of six or eight to squabble over one disinterested hen. Perhaps the prize goes to the one that can display the most exaggerated visage to its fellows: histrionics in action, the actor's craft defined.

Appearance aside, the harlequin leads a rugged life. Its circumpolar distribution consigns it to the coldest seas in the hemisphere, and when it ventures inland it proves uniquely adapted to swift, tumbling currents that support few other divers. When I was exploring the Siberian wilderness 20 years ago, I frequently encountered inland harlequins in one of the world's harshest environments. Their diet consists almost exclusively of fish and crustaceans, and in Alaska I've spent hours watching them ambush outbound salmon smolt during the spring. Their carnivorous habits make them a challenge in the kitchen, but I once won a cooking contest in camp by serving harlequin duck glazed with ginger. It is possible to render them tasty, given a bit of imagination.

But that wasn't what I had in mind that morning on Kodiak. Heads and horns adorn the inside of our house, the legacy of a lifetime squandered with a longbow, but at the time I'd never sent any waterfowl to the taxidermist. I couldn't think of a better initial subject than a harlequin.

Really wanting to kill one specific bird has a nasty habit of inducing bad shooting, and I felt grateful that the harlequins—which decoy more enthusiastically than most sea ducks—were almost to the shoreline when they finally flared. Aware of my interests, Ernie courteously conceded the flock to me, which only added to the pressure. But the lead drake fell on schedule, and Yaeger quickly turned the retrieve into another advertisement for his breed.

Today, a thousand miles from the sea, I can still look at that mounted bird's clownish face and remember the wind and the rain, and the wilderness the harlequin calls home.

Kenai with a Washington coast widgeon.

CHAPTER SIXTEEN

Squeakers

NOTHING CONFIRMS ARRIVAL in the wilderness like the sound of a floatplane's departure in the Alaska bush. Fifteen minutes earlier we'd been soaring high above the tundra ourselves, and then we were unloading dogs and decoys, and then, well… there we were, alone in a vast silence broken only by the sound of geese calling from the nearby Bristol Bay tide line. But the geese could wait; we had ducks to deal with first.

After pausing to appreciate the delicious loneliness of our surroundings, we went to work. We'd barely finished pitching a dozen blocks onto the pond's surface when another sound arose somewhere high and behind us, a liquid three-note whistle that sounded oddly musical in contrast to the harsh cries from the distant geese. "Widgeons!" I whispered to Lori, and then we were all diving for cover in the grass.

Few puddle ducks decoy as reliably or gracefully as widgeons, and by the time I'd chambered a pair of shells the flock of a dozen birds had turned onto short final approach, cupped their wings, and fought the gusting breeze down toward the middle of the decoys. The shooting was quick and elegant rather than technically challenging, and then it was time to call for Harley, our friend Alex's yellow Lab. He had barely completed the first retrieve by the time I heard more widgeons in the air behind us, but we didn't even bother to interrupt the dog work. Flocks of birds were circling every quadrant of the sky, and I already knew we were in for the kind of morning only widgeons can provide.

Many seasons have passed since I saw my first widgeon, but I still remember the event clearly even though I was only five or six years old at the time. Already armed with my own pair of hand-me-down binoculars, I was watching a scattered assortment of ducks on a suburban Boston reservoir when an unfamiliar specimen caught my eye. "What's that one?" I asked my mother.

"Let's look it up in the bird book," she replied, for she had already learned that teaching me how to answer my own questions was a better method of instruction than answering them for me.

Our vintage reference actually identified the bird as a baldpate, which required a bit of explanation since I had no idea what a pate was. While the breeding male's prominent white crown made a practical field mark, it was the species' voice rather than any element of its plumage that eventually impressed me as distinctive. I might have called the birds whistlers, but the goldeneye had already laid claim to that nickname. I finally settled on "squeakers" in my own private vocabulary, since the widgeon's call reminded me of the squeaking noise a child's toy animal makes when compressed.

Early in my waterfowling career widgeons were rare visitors to our Atlantic Flyway decoys spreads, but when my family moved to Washington State we began to encounter them frequently. I quickly learned to enjoy the species for its beauty, table quality, and willingness to decoy, an appreciation undiminished by time. When I moved out to the plains of Montana, widgeons were "dime" birds in the old Central Flyway point system, and I learned to shoot them selectively, along with pintails and blue-wings, so I could go home with 10 birds hanging from my duck strap rather than eating up my limit with 20-point mallard drakes. Just imagine… but that was a long time ago.

One morning during my medical residency days in Seattle, a friend and I were returning from a steelhead outing on the Skykomish River when we noticed large flocks of ducks circling a damp pasture that didn't look like waterfowl habitat at all. A polite visit to the nearest farmhouse secured us permission to shoot the field, and we returned later that afternoon with shotguns, decoys, and my first great Lab, appropriately named Skykomish. After several seasons spent hunting in solitude on the Montana prairie the noise of traffic in the distance proved distracting, but the number of ducks in the air quickly erased whatever reservations I felt about hunting close to civilization.

The birds all turned out to be widgeons. The sound of their individual calls combined to fill the air with a monotonous hum that sounded like mosquitoes swarming about my ears. With nothing but an irrigation ditch for a blind, we collected easy limits of decoying birds and then stayed until dark just to watch the show. Experiences like that can create a soft spot in the heart for any quarry.

In the interest of accuracy I should note that the species' full common name is the American widgeon, which implies the presence of another variety, as indeed there is. One of our more common stray waterfowl from the Old World, the Eurasian widgeon visits occasionally along both our coasts. I've never been fortunate enough to see one, but I'm still looking.

Back along that tundra pothole, the shooting quickly aroused memories of the unlikely hunt I'd enjoyed in Washington four decades earlier. The setting and circumstances could not have been more different, but the star of the show was just the same. As the wind freshened from the sea, birds just kept coming while Lori and I traded shotgun and camera back and forth. By the time we finally picked up the blocks and began to slog across the tundra to mount a campaign against the geese, limits of ducks lay on top of the decoy bag, all but three of them widgeons.

The genus *Anas* includes all the North American puddle ducks except for the woody and the two whistling ducks, and the widgeon's full scientific name, *Anas americana*, suggests that the widgeon, rather than the mallard, really should be our iconic national dabbler. It doesn't take many outings like the one we enjoyed that morning on the Alaska Peninsula to leave me convinced.

So let's hear it for the squeaker.

Bowdoin NWR in June.

CHAPTER SEVENTEEN

Off Season

IT'S SUMMERTIME, and the living is easy… That's not always the case as we shall see, but this evening Gershwin seems to have nailed it. It's early June on northern Montana's Bowdoin National Wildlife Refuge, and the mosquitoes have yet to make their first serious appearance of the season. Although my watch and my stomach agree that the hour is growing late, the summer sun still hangs well above the prairie horizon to the west, promising enduring light for our camera. And spread out before us lies yet another promise fulfilled: the abundance and diversity of wildlife nature can produce from dry terrain given a bit of water with which to work.

While an abundance of waterfowl never fails to move me, it's their diversity that offers the main attraction tonight. In less than an hour, Lori and I have identified almost every species of duck known to breed in the Central Flyway. While there's nothing unusual about the mallards and gadwalls, they still evoke the warm familiarity of old friends. The sight of all those pintails and blue-wings feels especially gratifying, since both are favorite species whose populations have struggled recently. Then there are the divers; cans, redheads, and scaup are never common visitors on the small water we hunt close to home. Plentiful spoonbills remind me that a drake shoveler in breeding plumage is one of the most spectacular birds on the prairie. Finally, the edges of the reeds teem with ruddy ducks, and the strikingly marked males staring back at me over their blue bills look like visitors from another galaxy.

Bowdoin lies just far enough from our home to put it out of reach for a casual autumn duck hunt. But tonight, after a long day's work at the clinic on the nearby Fort Belknap Reservation, I can't imagine a place I'd rather be.

Duck seasons run from September through January in various parts of the country, but most serious hunters I know find ways to make their fascination with waterfowl last twelve months a year. Waterfowl related activities during the traditional off-season may be as casual as attending a DU banquet mid-winter or visiting with a friendly landowner in the spring about leaving an extra margin of cover around a pothole when it's time to cut hay. They may also be as involved as committing time to a habitat project in the field over the course of the summer. Point is, the birds are there year around, and one way or another we should be too.

I've always enjoyed spending time in duck country over the summer, when the birds are dressed in their finest and pleasant weather makes all time spent indoors feel squandered. While "scouting" offers a great excuse, the inevitable shuffling of the deck before hunting season opens renders that fiction difficult to sustain. That's why Lori and I love to carry our cameras along to places like Bowdoin. Waterfowl make challenging subjects for wildlife photographers, but even though most of our own images wind up in the digital trash heap, obtaining them provides a reason to be out in the wetlands smelling the mud.

But not all of my off-season summertime waterfowl expeditions fall under the heading of easy living. Back when I lived right in the heart of prairie pothole country nearly 40 years ago, my hunting partners and I spent countless late summer evenings building blinds in new locations wherever water and habitat conditions looked most promising. That meant lugging heavy loads of fence posts, wire, and lumber across miles of mud while the dogs splattered us with pond water, sweat ran down our necks, and mosquitoes tried to drain our last drops of blood.

One afternoon we decided that we could eliminate some heavy packing by driving my pickup along the edge of a marsh to the waterline where we'd decided to erect a new blind. All went well for several hundred yards, at which point the truck's wheels broke through the crust of dry mud beneath them and left us bogged down to the frame. Recognizing that we weren't going to extricate ourselves under our own power even with a winch and chains, I hiked back down the road to the nearest ranch house.

I only meant to call back to town for reinforcements, but when I described our predicament the rancher figured he could pull us out with his tractor. Unfortunately, we'd been even stupider than he imagined. "You boys sure must love to hunt ducks," he declared back at the scene of the disaster. But an hour later, we'd rounded up enough rope, cable, and chain from the farmyard to stretch from the sinking rig to his tractor on solid ground. After popping the truck out of the mud like a cork, he invited us back to his house for dinner with his family. Now whenever the conversation turns to the good old days, I still remember that afternoon.

Back at Bowdoin, Lori and I have let our attention wander beyond duck stamp subjects to the rest of the marsh's inhabitants: Wilson's phalaropes, marbled godwits, black-necked stilts, and finally white-faced ibises of all things, way out here on the Montana prairie. The lesson is obvious: what's good for ducks is good for a host of other wildlife as well. As we return to the vehicle and ease on down the road, magpies erupt from the grass beside us. A quick investigation reveals an antelope fawn that didn't survive its first day on the ground. A coyote's victim? Probably, but what does that matter? As Aldo Leopold noted, wild places cannot have room for one without having room for all.

As the light drains from the sky and we reach pavement at last, I face a final realization. There is no such thing as an off-season for those who care about waterfowl, nor should there be.

Yellow-headed blackbird.
Wetlands restoration benefits countless non-game species.

Section II

In the Field: Ducks

Lori and Rocky with a limit of late season mallards.

In the Field: Ducks

MOST WATERFOWLERS begin their careers hunting ducks, and many end them without ever hunting anything else. Little wonder; despite the drama of goose hunting, America's duck population holds enough mystery and challenge (not to mention great eating) to keep even the most dedicated outdoors enthusiast enthralled for a lifetime.

Depending on whether one is a lumper or a splitter, some three dozen species of ducks breed on our continent and this figure does not include the accidentals and strays from the Old World that find their way to our shores from both directions. Ignoring the like of ruddy ducks, whistling ducks, and mergansers, most can be classified as dabblers, divers, or sea ducks. Each of the three genres enjoys its own long tradition of craft and lore related to its pursuit. Like most inland hunters I spend most of my time with the dabblers, but I have never been one to play favorites, and if the chance arises to pursue goldeneyes or bluebills I'll jump at it. As noted, I have friends and hunting partners who would be happy to shoot nothing but drake mallards for the rest of their lives, but I've always felt that a broad sampling from the menu helps make me a more complete outdoorsman.

Duck hunting has exerted a peculiar hold on me ever since my early childhood, and I've never shaken its allure. I've traveled the world with my longbow in pursuit of big game and spent nearly as much time on wilderness waters with my fly rod, but I remain a bird hunter at heart. Even within the wide domain of wing-shooting, ducks have always exerted a special appeal. As much as I love the physical exertion, challenging shooting, and exciting dog work an upland hunt in my home states of

Montana and Alaska can provide, nothing can rival the ambience of a duck blind at dawn, the enthusiasm of a retriever crashing through icy water, or the spectacle of a wary pintail flock setting its wings and descending toward the decoys. Perhaps the measured pace of a typical duck hunt simply gives the hunter more time to appreciate what hurtles by too quickly during the pursuit of other feathered game.

And as it happens, I love to eat duck. While my family subsists largely on wild game of all kinds, nothing excites me as much in the kitchen or on the table as a prime mallard, pintail, or teal. Regrettably, not all duck hunters share my enthusiasm for the real thing, and every season lots of fine dining needlessly gets converted to sausage, jerky, and other culinary abominations just because too many duck hunters have not learned to cook what they shoot. To the extent that this volume contains any agenda other than the celebration of wildlife and its habitat, it's convincing other hunters to learn to enjoy eating ducks.

Volumes have been written on the practical aspects of hunting ducks, from decoys to calls to the selection of guns and loads. While experience has left me with strong opinions on many of those subjects, I remain happy to leave their elucidation to others. The notes that follow are meant to address the why rather than the how, and if I have done my job the reader will go away with nothing more than a heightened curiosity about the endlessly fascinating world of duck hunting.

Opening day on the Montana prairie.

Alaska Peninsula widgeons on a breezy day.

CHAPTER EIGHTEEN

Winds of Fortune

I FELT THE TRUCK ROCKING in the crosswind as we drove down the highway in the dark, and by the time we reached our destination, I could barely open the door against its force. I hadn't visited the slough in several weeks and wasn't even sure it contained any open water after a recent cold snap, but the gray light revealed wavelets breaking over the ice along its edges. "This is terrible!" my hunting partner, a novice waterfowler, observed as the gale tore away his shooting vest before he could buckle it to his body. On the contrary, I assured him. This was perfect.

Fifteen minutes later, we sat huddled in a clump of brush beside a minimalist spread of a dozen decoys, each tacking crazily back and forth against its anchor line as if it meant to sprout real wings and fly. A few more knots of southwest chinook wind spilling down across the mountains' eastern slope likely would have overturned them, but the anchors held and they all managed to stay upright somehow, not that events let us worry about them for long.

I hadn't even loaded my gun when Rocky's face turned skyward, a cue I've learned can only mean one thing. Inbound from a nearby stubble field, a large flight of mallards was rocketing through the downwind leg of an approach to the slough. "Ready?" I hissed to my partner as I fumbled a pair of shells into my double. I'm not sure what I would have done had he told me that he wasn't.

The birds offered a spectacular performance on their final descent. Fighting the wind all the way, two hundred of them banked into the turn, cupped their wings, and slid downward in slow motion. Transfixed, I nearly forgot to stand and shoot, but suddenly we had greenheads hanging right in front of our faces. "Take 'em!" I cried, and the two of us rose to do just that.

Hitting ducks riding a stiff tailwind poses technical difficulties of its own, but paradoxically, floaters can be even tougher. There is a natural tendency to stare and point instead of putting your face down on the stock and swinging the shotgun, and experienced shots all know the results of such breakdowns in fundamentals. By the time I isolated a drake from the flock, the birds were starting to flare, and as that bird folded, the rest turned, caught the wind, and sailed out of range before I could think about my second barrel.

Not that it mattered. Two limits of mallards were obviously going to fall from the sky that morning, thanks to a good set up, being in the right place at the right time, and a little help from the wind.

Homer's Odyssey begins with a spiteful Aeolus, the Greek god of winds, scattering the heroes' ships across the Aegean: no wind, no epic. In the era of sailing vessels, the only thing worse than too much breeze may have been not enough, as captured in Patrick O'Brien's descriptions of becalmed ships in his splendid seafaring novels. All of which proves that sailors may be almost as hard to please in matters of weather as Montana farmers.

But waterfowlers feel no such ambiguity. More wind translates into better duck hunting, almost without exception. Breezes make decoy spreads come to life, inviting attention from high-flying ducks overhead. Strong winds keep birds from rafting up in open water far from shore, beyond the reach of decoys, calls, and other stratagems. Calm days may make time pass more comfortably in the blind, but if comfort were their highest priority, duck hunters would never leave their cozy homes in the first place. Hence the momentary dissonance between my inexperienced partner and me that morning: He only knew how the wind felt, while I knew what it promised.

And the wind kept that promise. By the time the third flock entered the familiar traffic pattern overhead, I wasn't even bothering to load my second barrel. I told myself I was indulging this exercise in restraint so I could concentrate on working the dog, but in fact I just didn't want the spectacle to end any sooner than necessary. For nearly an hour, the wind kept howling and the birds kept arriving to fight their way down to the slough. We rose and shot when we couldn't stand it any longer, and Rocky scooped up mallards and delivered them like early Christmas presents. Finally, we had ten greenheads lying in the snow beside us and the hunting was over, although we still had birds trying to land on our heads as we picked up the blocks and prepared to head reluctantly back to town.

And in the Homeric tradition, I sent a small burnt offering (a gizzard) skyward when I cooked the ducks on the grill that night. The day belonged to Aeolus, and it only seemed proper to express my gratitude.

Yaeger and Bob May at Whale Pass, Alaska.

CHAPTER NINETEEN

The Eider Sanction

AS WE LIFTED OFF across Cook Inlet, a mosaic of clotted ice pans slid beneath the wing: a winter landscape by Jackson Pollock, chaotic yet oddly serene. The air outside looked cold enough to bite back hard. We were all veterans of countless expeditions to Kodiak, but this was December, the season of long nights and unforgiving weather, and the last of our common sense rudely reminded us how easy it would have been to find a more comfortable way to spend the week.

The mission felt as unconventional as our timing. We were hunting eiders, the north's largest, most mysterious sea ducks. I should retract my use of the plural, since I only wanted one. You don't hunt eiders to fill the larder. You hunt them because they are there. Maybe.

The following morning, we awoke at our friend Bob May's cabin to find a calm sea licking lazily at fresh snow along the shoreline. Despite the gorgeous winter scenery our spirits sank, since eiders remain content to ride the waves offshore under all but the most punishing conditions at sea. This principle results in a meteorological Catch-22: if the weather is nice enough to make eider hunting reasonable, there probably won't be any eiders. After breakfast, we exchanged shotguns for bows and set off through the fresh snow, and by early afternoon, I had a young blacktail buck hanging behind the cabin.

The following morning presented similar weather conditions and more inertia on the part of the waterfowl, and we changed our agenda again. This time our alternative quarry waited deep beneath the slick, gray sea. I can think of one good reason why the idea of winter halibut fishing in Kodiak waters sounds crazy: it is. As we boarded the skiff, I tried to ignore the chunks of ice clinging to the cabin. When Bob cut the power out in the pass, I sent a heavy jig plummeting into the darkness below and settled back to glass for eiders while we fished.

A circumpolar family of sea ducks splendidly adapted to the arctic maritime environment, eiders don't enjoy a lot of contact with people. Perhaps that's just as well for them. Prized for the quality of their down, eiders were commercially harvested to near extinction in the Atlantic before more enlightened management policies allowed populations to recover. Four species inhabit Alaska, of which two–the spectacled and Steller's–remain too rare to hunt. While there are plenty of commons and kings, I only wanted one drake for the taxidermist, to remind me of the spell cast by the wild and lonely places eiders call home.

That night, wind began to rock the cabin, and the following morning we watched the distant sun burn its way through the storm's lingering scud until it flooded the hills with the eerie light unique to Alaska on crisp winter days. Fighting against the tide, a stiff gale churned the pass to froth, leaving Bob's skiff tossing like a bronco on its running line. Finally: eider hunting weather.

Too a fault, in fact. We needed to cover lots of water in search of our elusive quarry, but nothing could have convinced us to put out in that sea. Finally, Ernie Holland and I shouldered decoy bags and set off on foot toward a beach a mile away with Yaeger, Bob's seaworthy Chessie, at heel. Meanwhile, Bob and Denny Daigger wisely volunteered to work on the woodpile. We quickly realized who'd wound up with the better end of that deal.

Angry surf and scattered flocks of scoters and harlequins waited for us at the beach. The gale cut us to the marrow and driven spray quickly glazed our outerwear. After untangling a rat's nest of frozen lines, we pitched a handful of decoys toward the slick spot just beyond the breaking surf and settled in to wait.

Sunlight sparkled from snow-clad peaks and the driven sea seemed alive with energy. A rich variety of North Pacific bird life lay scattered across the bay: dagger-billed loons, strikingly patterned harlequins, and rhinoceros auklets bobbing through the waves. But there were no eiders.

Hiking in bitter weather is one thing, but letting cold digest you at rest is another. The surf and dropping tide seemed determined to reject our decoy spread. When we walked down to pitch the washed-up blocks back into the sea, a wave caught me as I bent down to untangle a line, sending frigid seawater over my boots. Finally, we had to admit we'd reached our limits. Chilled and disconsolate, we gathered our gear and set off toward the cabin's distant comfort.

We eventually left Kodiak without a single glimpse of our quarry. But we survived, and in Alaska it's sometimes wise to settle for a draw. On any hunt, making the process the focus of the experience eliminates most elements of disappointment. From that perspective, there will always be another season, and time for another quest.

By the time we settled back to the tarmac in Anchorage, we were already thinking about next year.

Prairie sunrise. Don and Rocky on the Rez.

CHAPTER TWENTY

First Light

I **KNOW A LITTLE POTHOLE** hidden away in the eastern Montana prairie. It isn't much as wetlands go: a few acres of mud and marsh barely big enough to attract the teal that have always provided an excuse to visit. But it's one of the best places I know to begin the day, especially in early October during the magical interlude between summer's heat and the arrival of real winter weather, when the air has just started to turn crisp. At that time of year, daybreak there feels like a dream refracted through a perfect celestial lens. Visitors with the patience to look carefully will enjoy an opportunity to see the world as few others ever will.

On that lonely stretch of grass and sage, vast miles of nothing stand between the observer and the sunrise, creating the illusion of being at sea. Of course the sun doesn't really rise at all; our planet's eastern edge bows to meet it. I know no better place to appreciate the truth of how sunrises really work. And when that bright solar disc finally crests the distant horizon, it always looks at least three sizes too big, a phenomenon one regular hunting partner and I have argued about for years. He says optical illusion created by figure-ground relationship, I say distortion of light rays transmitted through more layers of atmosphere, and in the end we both usually wind up sounding like fools who don't know nearly as much about the world as we think. On the good days, the teal arrive in time to shut us up, for which we both thank them even when we miss.

A lone cottonwood stands on the eastern side of the little marsh, across the water from the reeds where I usually set up my blind: the only tree for miles around. Smacked by lightning and ravaged by too many years of drought, its best years clearly lie behind it, but after watching the early light filter through those defiant branches more times than I can count, I've come to think of the cottonwood as my own personal National Forest. The tree must have meant something special to someone else as well, for the remains of an old homesteader's cabin lie scattered nearby. And I have to wonder how many times whoever built it stopped toiling long enough to enjoy the same sunrise before he dried up and went bust.

That ruined building illustrates a curious point. Relentless as the press of human development often seems, it's still possible to find places apparently immune to the mixed blessings of progress. Of course, you have to look hard these days to find them. I note with interest how often the pursuit of waterfowl has shown me the way and how much more intriguing those special places always look in the first light of day.

Waterfowling may be the most visually compelling of all outdoor sports. Painters and photographers have celebrated this realization for years, creating an artistic tradition unrivaled anywhere else in the wide world of fish and game. Interesting subject matter has certainly helped the cause, as anyone who has watched a flock of mallards spiral downward into a decoy spread can attest. But waterfowl enjoy another important advantage over other outdoor subjects. Ducks and geese are creatures of first light, when the busy world sleeps and nature looks her best. Whether they choose to express themselves with oils, watercolors, or film, waterfowl artists don't have to manufacture romantic settings for their subjects. The birds take care of that, as I realize every time I watch a flight of teal silhouetted against the sunrise over that little pothole.

Duck hunting means many things to many people. I still enjoy the challenge of the shooting, the drama of the dogs, the companionship of friends, and the rich bounty of wild game on the table. But like all of life's enduring mysteries, duck hunting manages somehow to add up to more than the sum of its parts. In the busy modern world, less really can mean more, especially when you've earned the right to enjoy it by rising early and walking far. Friends lament that we're raising a generation of urban children who have never seen a wild bird or animal, a deficiency with obvious implications for the future of wildlife. But the real problem may be even more basic. Growing up in a world of manmade horizons and artificial light, they've never even seen a sunrise, not the way I have, with pure light overhead and clean dirt underfoot and a dozen teal inbound toward the blind and the hunter's heart.

They need to know these things. I wish I could show them all, just the way the teal showed me.

Set up for teal on the Texas Gulf Coast.

CHAPTER TWENTY-ONE

A Matter of Style

MID-AFTERNOON one breezy but surprisingly balmy November day, Lori and I set off to slog through a quarter mile of old snow to a slough where I felt confident we'd enjoy furious shooting at last light. Kenai was a big puppy then, and Lori had her hands full managing him on his leash. Meanwhile, I forged ahead with the decoy bag over one shoulder, wondering if anyone has ever designed a load more awkward to carry and appreciating Rocky's good manners as he followed dutifully at heel.

The pool where we planned to set up lay under a steep bank, and a great commotion arose as we crested it. Forty mallards sat tucked in beneath its lee and all of them flushed at once, filling the air with noise and wings at point blank range. Instinctively, I dropped the decoys and shouldered my shotgun… only to hold my fire and stare at the spectacle of the departing birds.

"Why didn't you shoot?" Lori asked as Kenai finished dragging her to my side.

Good question…

I've certainly jump-shot my share of waterfowl over the years and had a lot of fun (and eaten a lot of ducks) as a result. As a kid, I not infrequently invested as much strategy and effort sneaking up on ponds that contained a teal or two as I do nowadays stalking big game with my bow. Later in my career, I taught Skykomish, my first great Lab, to slink along behind me on jump-shoots with his profile lowered like a cat stalking a robin on the lawn.

Some of those belly-crawling escapades proved as spectacular as anything I've ever experienced in a duck blind, like the time my hunting partner returned to the truck after scouting a prairie stock pond and gleefully reported a flock of mallards nestled beneath the dam. After making a long circle through the sage, we crested the rise only to find that the dozen mallards had morphed into 200 honkers, all of which took to the air right in front of our faces. What a show that turned out to be, for guns and dogs alike.

But most of my jump shooting days lie behind me now, a dry fly vs. nymph matter of personal preference with no moral judgment involved. Nothing wrong with the old sneak and jump, mind you. I've just learned that I now prefer to shoot my ducks in other ways.

There are practical reasons why I declined that splendid shooting opportunity last November. I knew that if left undisturbed, the ducks would have no reason to distinguish me from the rancher checking his cows, and that they would likely filter back to the slough and our decoys in singles and pairs… which they did at last shooting light. But that still doesn't completely explain my failure to fire.

I've become addicted to the grand spectacle of ducks spiraling into decoys. I admit my infatuation with every aspect of the drama: the strategy of the spread, the music of the calls, the companionship of the dogs as we huddle together in wait. And then there is the artistry of the birds in the air: teal, mallards, pintails, and divers, each approaching with their characteristic signature of wing-beats against the distant glow of the sun. Never mind the bird book; this is how duck hunters know their ducks, and over the years I've developed the discipline to sacrifice a lot of easy shooting in order to experience waterfowl as I enjoy them most.

None of which means that I've jump-shot my last duck.

Chances are I'll crawl on my belly a time or two next season, because we have friends or family coming over for a duck dinner, one of the young dogs needs a retrieve, or for the best reason of all: it's still fun, even after all these years.

But when it comes time to go duck hunting, as opposed to meat gathering, dog training or just being a kid again, I'll do it the way I've grown to love, even when that means rising in the dark, hiking through snow-covered fields, and wrestling with frozen decoy lines. That choice won't be a function of pretension, correctness, or laziness in the face of hundred-yard crawls through snow or mud. It will just be a matter of style.

So what was the real reason I didn't drop an easy pair of greenheads from that dramatic rise over the slough? I knew which way the wind was blowing. I knew there would be ducks tucked beneath the bank.

That's why my shotgun wasn't loaded.

Don and Rocky at 10-below.

CHAPTER TWENTY-TWO

Blizzard Season

THE STORM STRUCK after Christmas, filling the valley with a whole winter's worth of fury. Lori and I hunkered down inside and watched the wind sculpt fresh snow into monstrous drifts that prevented any possibility of travel. The kids were home for the holidays but the storm had left them stranded in town with friends, so the dogs provided our only company. Years in Alaska taught me the wisdom of accepting weather rather than fighting it, and for two days we enjoyed the peace and quiet and let the storm run its course.

But by Day Three I was starting to feel confined, especially since I knew the weather would have the mallards concentrated on whatever open water remained: a catalog of spring-fed creeks and ponds I've spent decades finding. I skied the worst mile of the road leading down through the hills from our house and decided I could make it in the truck with some effort and planning. But as I finished putting the chains on all four tires, the radio announced that every road in the county was limited to emergency travel only. I placed a call to a friend in law enforcement and asked if the definition of emergency included a desperate need to hunt ducks. That earned a laugh and the promise of a ticket if he saw me on a public road, so I spent the afternoon pitching dummies into the snow for the puppy.

Travel restrictions lifted the following day. A bitter arctic high had arrived on the storm's heels and the thermometer registered five below despite brilliant sunshine overhead. Lori told me flat out that duck hunting sounded crazy. No matter; I was going anyway. Shortly after noon, I kenneled Rocky in the back of the truck and blasted off through three feet of virgin snow.

An hour later, I pulled up to a friend's farmhouse and found no one home. During cold snaps, ducks often gather in a creek bend near the feedlot behind the house. The rancher knows me well enough to have given me standing permission to hunt there even with cattle nearby. But as I crested the bank, my spirits sank. The weather had sealed the whole creek in ice so thick that cows were walking across it without breaking through.

Floundering through drifts up to my waist, I checked two more likely spots on the creek without finding any open water. Just as I was about to give up, I heard the unmistakable chuckle of mallards in the distance. When I finally localized the sound, I realized it was coming from a small spring a mile to the south. But when I started the truck again and set off in that direction, I promptly wound up mired to my axles and extricated myself only with difficulty.

I then faced a dilemma. The track was hopelessly drifted in, but open ground lay to the side and with wheat stubble tops visible all the way, I knew enough snow had blown off the field for me to drive it. The ground was frozen and nothing but stubble lay beneath the snow, but I have a firm rule against driving anywhere off-road on private property without specific permission. I knew I'd receive it if my friends were home, but they weren't. Reluctantly, I slung the decoy bag over my shoulder and set off into the face of a freshening wind.

The slog across the field proved cold and brutal, but when Rocky and I reached the spring, hundreds of mallards exploded in front of us. To Rocky's consternation, I just stood in silence and let the air beneath all those straining wings wash over us as the birds rose and dispersed. By the time I had the decoys on the water, only an hour of shooting light remained.

More than enough, as events soon proved… As we settled into the brush, birds began to filter back in singles and pairs, the drakes' green heads gleaming in the crisp afternoon light. The shooting was all close range kid stuff and I quickly had a limit resting beside me. I unloaded and tried to take some pictures, but my camera was frozen and I finally had to acknowledge that I was too. The lone dissenter, Rocky plainly would have stayed and fetched until the spring (or hell itself) froze over, but he didn't get to vote.

"I can't believe you went hunting today!" Lori said when I finally walked back through the door. "That was crazy!"

"It wasn't crazy," I corrected her. "It was an emergency."

Late season on the Kodiak Coast.

CHAPTER TWENTY-THREE

The Scent of the Sea

KODIAK ISLAND, ALASKA: dull November skies overhead, the gentle slap of waves against the gravel beach, a dozen magnum decoys tacking back and forth against the current 20 yards beyond our makeshift driftwood blind. The pervasive saline scent of the North Pacific permeates the air, reflected from the organic debris the last high tide left behind, the bottoms of our boots where cold salt mud still clings, and Yaeger, Bob May's hardy Chesapeake Bay retriever. Absent too long from the tide line, I close my eyes and drink in the smell of the place. For the moment at least, the ducks can wait.

From crab legs to commerce, the sea has always helped define the Alaska experience... and the development of American waterfowling traditions. While most modern duck hunters practice their craft away from the marine environment, we all owe a historical debt to the saltwater marshes along our eastern seaboard, which produced a legacy ranging from our great retrieving breeds to the finest examples of the decoy carver's art.

My own fascination with hunting ducks at sea began four decades ago when I was growing up near Puget Sound. While my family made plenty of trips across the Cascades to enjoy classic puddle duck hunting in the Columbia basin, our less frequent waterfowling excursions on salt water quickly earned a special place in my heart. On the good days near the mouth of Hood Canal and Sequim Bay, we shot black brant, graceful pelagic birds that captured my imagination the way tall ships at dockside must have captured boys' imaginations two centuries earlier. The rest of the time we shot what came by (goldeneye, bufflehead, scoter) and timed the long walk back along the beach to coincide with low tide so we could stuff ourselves with freshly shucked oysters. Even when the birds ignored our decoys and skimmed past out of range, there were always things to see, and the smell of the ocean inevitably lingered when Monday rolled around and I trudged back to school.

When I moved to Alaska in 1980, Cook Inlet's tide flats provided a waterfowling venue unlike any I'd ever seen before. While the pace of the actual shooting ranged from slow to furious, I'd be hard pressed to recount a boring day spent at the cabin my friends and I maintained on the Inlet's wild western shore. With huge tides on one side and towering volcanic peaks on the other, hunts there always felt greater than the ducks they produced even on the best days.

As all sailors know, the sea can prove a cruel mistress. We fretted over dogs in cold water and slogged through long miles of frigid tidal muck. One evening, we dallied a little too long and returned to the beach to discover that the combination of unusually high tide and stiff southeast wind had left our Super Cubs bobbing around in the surf like bathtub toys. A year ago during a combination deer and duck hunt on Kodiak Island, two friends and I punctured the hull of our inflatable boat on a floating ice pan and enjoyed the coldest, scariest swim of our lives. But I wouldn't have missed any of it for the world. Well, almost any of it…

Back in our lonely beachfront hiding place, Yaeger has started to fidget. As endlessly patient in a blind as he is tenacious in the water, he's not a dog to squirm without reason. Aroused by his sudden intensity, I open my eyes in time to see a flock of surf scoters round the nearest point and veer toward the blocks. Even after 40 years of sea duck hunting the outlandish white-crested males look exotic, like refugees from another continent. But this is what we've come to do and by the time we've stood and done it four birds lie kicking in the chop and Yaeger is steaming out to meet them. And when he's done we've added these smells to the potpourri: the tang of burnt powder, the rich organic aroma of the birds, the splendid stink of more wet Chessie than most of us should ever care to know.

The Big Show: Alberta geese.

CHAPTER TWENTY-FOUR

The Big Show

THE WEATHER THAT AFTERNOON defined Indian summer on the high plains. Although more October lay behind us on the calendar than ahead, the air still felt muggy enough to make us sweat inside our waders on the long hike out through the marsh. Once we'd finished setting up, the decoys looked inert and lifeless on the slick water, and for nearly two hours nothing stirred but the last of the season's bugs. Even the dogs were looking disinterested by the time a lonely pair of ducks appeared silhouetted against the distant azure sky. The birds turned out to be shovelers, but we rose and killed them anyway when they turned to circle the spread. Finally, Dick and I acknowledged defeat and began to gather the decoys just ahead of final shooting light.

But a funny thing happened on our way back to the truck. Fumbling to balance shotgun and decoy bag, I heard the unmistakable whistle of wings rise above the sloshing noise of our boots, and when I looked up the sky was full of ducks. With no decoy spread and no cover other than sparse marsh grass, the birds had no reason to pass within shotgun range, but they did anyway. By the time we'd dropped the decoys and fumbled through our vests for shells, they'd settled into the grass around us before we could shoot.

As I finally located a pair of shells, I heard still more birds on the wing behind us. Pivoting in that direction, I realized that the first set had been nothing but the leading edge of the spectacle. Wave after wave of birds, all plump northern mallards, turned in endless vortices against the dying light behind them. Just like that, the once listless skies above the marsh had decided to treat us to ringside seat at the Big Show.

I've always been amazed by the way waterfowling's pace can vary. While it's probably possible to calculate some kind of mathematical average, there's really no such thing as a typical day of duck hunting. My waterfowl harvest survey data always boils down to guesswork, because I've never believed in keeping score even for scientific purposes. Some days a lot of ducks appear and cooperate while others offer hardly any. The trick is to find a way to enjoy them all, even if you've spent a long, hot afternoon swatting bugs just to shoot a pair of spoonbills.

But some days of duck hunting cross a qualitative line between great shooting and the phenomenon I call the Big Show. Don't fret over definitions: Like art or obscenity, you'll know it when you see it. Numbers only tell part of the story. To qualify, the birds should be close as well as plentiful. No doubt reflecting a safety-in-numbers attitude, they often wind up acting incautious if not downright crazy. And let no one kid you; we all live for it, even hunters like me who have found meaning in more uneventful mornings in the blind than most duck hunters will ever have to endure.

All kinds of ducks can participate. Mallards are obvious candidates because of their size and tendency to travel in large flocks. But I can also remember a still morning on another prairie marsh when the air filled with blue-wings staging for migration, offering a version of the Big Show that flocks of greenheads would be hard pressed to rival.

Appreciating the Big Show has surprisingly little to do with shooting ducks. Shotguns only hold so many shells, and once two or three birds appear in range, the contribution to the bag won't vary whether the rest of the flock contains one bird or one thousand. Not that it matters; the Big Show is something that happens to you rather than the other way around.

Back on that lonely northeastern Montana marsh, Dick and I independently reached the same conclusion. No doubt we could have quickly killed limits in the last few minutes of light as the birds descended, but we unloaded our guns instead. Initially boisterous to the threshold of control, even the dogs finally stood in silence as wings brushed past our faces in the gathering gloom. Frankly, I'd never seen anything like it.

I assume no moral high ground because of the decision to hold our fire. I love to shoot and eat ducks as much as anyone. In the end, credit for our restraint goes to an odd combination of insight and self-interest. A quick limit of ducks would have been gone in a week, but we realized that we were witnessing a spectacle whose memory would endure far longer if only we'd give it the chance.

For even in a lifetime of waterfowling, one only receives so many invitations to the Big Show.

Diver decoys, looking for trouble.

CHAPTER TWENTY-FIVE

A Comedy
of Errors

As DISCUSSED in an earlier chapter about the Labrador duck, the extinction of a species usually depends on several unanticipated factors operating at once. The same principle holds when events unexpectedly go wrong for hunters in the field.

We don't get to hunt divers much at home in Montana, because there isn't enough big water nearby to hold them. During a recent visit to eastern Washington's Barker Ranch, a model Ducks Unlimited restoration project in which my parents hold an interest, Michael Crowder, the ranch's able young biologist, invited Lori and me to join him for an afternoon of serious diver hunting on the Columbia River. Since I hadn't shot a canvasback in years, I jumped at the chance.

Michael's small but seaworthy skiff was meticulously organized, with nearly a hundred decoys stuffed in pockets along the sides. Setting out the blocks was similar to setting long lines for halibut, a process I still remembered from my days as a commercial fisherman in Alaska. After some initial fumbling Lori and I had our part down, and we soon had four lines of artificial bluebills, goldeneyes, redheads, and cans bouncing in the chop. There were plenty of birds trading up and down the river. With waves of scaup breaking over us as we worked, we finished the last set and hurried around to drop anchor in position to receive the next arrivals.

That's when the first adverse event occurred: a sudden wind switch that left the decoys drifting into each other. We needed to reposition them quickly, so we motored around to the upwind side of the spread.

At which point we experienced our second unexpected difficulty: outboard motor failure. Directly upwind of the middle of the decoy lines, we couldn't have picked a worse place to lose power. With the motor shaft safely up out of the water, we still would have drifted harmlessly over the decoy lines except for (you guessed it) our third setback. Something on the hull, and we never determined what, hung down enough to snag the center of each main decoy line as we floated across them. This left us without power, in a wind rapidly freshening to a gale, drifting down the wide Columbia trailing hundreds of yards of line and dozens of decoys, all twisting rapidly into the Mother of All Messes.

Having faced my share of such snafu's over the years, I've developed my own approach to them. First and foremost, I ask a simple question: Have these unexpected developments placed us in danger? If the answer is affirmative, and I've learned to err on the conservative side, subsequent decisions take place under their own set of rules. While the wind, cold, and broad expanse of water ahead all made me pause and think, I concluded that we were safe, at least for the time being. The wind was blowing us toward shore, and with a shallow bar beneath us we could probably have walked the boat in if we had to.

So we dropped anchor and went to work on the motor. That problem proved embarrassingly simple to fix, and with power restored we all breathed a collective sigh of relief. Then we tackled the decoy tangle. Imagine picking a nasty backlash from a casting reel with an Argentine gaucho's bolas attached to the line every few feet. Three of the ground lines looked hopeless, but we eventually extracted the fourth along with two dozen free blocks. At that point, we made the only logical, responsible decision possible: we tied the tangle off on a stump and ran back up to the point to try to salvage a few birds from the last minutes of legal shooting light.

Cans were pouring down the river, and I really wanted a drake for the taxidermist. I had my chance too, but I missed. We were still able to drop enough bluebills to avoid the skunk, at which point we picked up the rest of our mess and headed home for hot showers and a well-earned Mexican dinner in nearby Richland.

Mallards were whistling through the half light overhead at the Barker Ranch when we arrived early the next morning, but we just couldn't leave Michael to face the leftover carnage alone. While he set off to oversee the morning's activities in the duck blinds, Lori and I hauled the frozen wreckage of the decoy spread out of the skiff and went to work. Years of experience with tangles involving everything from leaders to diamond hitches have left me philosophical about their apparent hopelessness in the beginning. Our goal, I explained to Lori, was to accomplish the mission without resorting to a knife or ending our marriage, and by mid-morning we'd done it.

We were laughing at ourselves too, and our laughter compensated for the canvasback drake I'd missed. Almost.

Kenai enjoying a fowl weather hunt.

CHAPTER TWENTY-SIX

Fowl Weather

WINDS: NORTHWEST 20, gusting to who knows what. Ceiling: indefinite. Visibility: one-quarter mile in sleet and drizzle. Dew point spread: nil. Temperature and barometer: both dropping like stones. Finally, after weeks of conventionally gorgeous Indian summer days, the weather feels perfect.

Perfect? Well yes, as a matter of fact. Clear skies and calm days may be fine for canoe trips or jaunts to the beach, but waterfowlers have always viewed the outdoors from their own loopy perspective. In the duck hunter's world, fair is foul and foul is fair as Shakespeare's witches famously observed, even if the concept may prove difficult for the uninitiated to appreciate.

Nothing illustrates the value of nasty weather to the duck hunter like its absence. Here on the high plains, the opening day of waterfowl season often arrives during shirtsleeve weather perfectly suited to working on a suntan. The despair during the slog out to the blind arises not from the annoying flies or the rivulets of sweat accumulating against the skin, but from the sight of all those ducks rafted up listlessly on the open water with no reason to fly. After all the anticipation accumulated over the long off-season, the feeling of futility can be enough to break the toughest heart. No wonder October's first serious cold front provides such a sense of relief, even if one's gratitude is better kept to oneself, at least in polite company.

With calm, clear skies overhead, ducks often stop looking like ducks as the hunter usually knows them. Reduced to inert, distant dots on a lake's mirrored surface, they lose their individuality, and when they finally take wing, flight usually occurs at stratospheric altitudes, with little or no attention paid to decoy spreads below. Contrast this sorry state of affairs with the excitement a shot of real weather can produce. Provide some wind and rain and the same lazy flocks will come alive, showing their colors as they wheel and circle on the breeze, suddenly attentive to decoy and call. No wonder duck blind veterans long for the kind of weather that makes their less lunatic neighbors retreat before the fireplace.

An important note: it is the perception of foul weather rather than the weather itself that causes discomfort in the field. Within reasonable limits, a duck hunter's notion of cold depends less on chill factor than on what the birds are doing. The arrival of a large flock of mallards over a decoy spread can confound the thermometer as if by magic, as we notice regularly on December duck hunts here on the High Plains. As a scientist, I'm not really sure how a few eager whines from a Labrador retriever and the feel of a shotgun against a shoulder can restore failing circulation to the extremities in seconds, but I appreciate this phenomenon every time it takes place. Never mind what the Weather Channel has to say about the kind of day ahead. Weather, like beauty, lies in the eye of the beholder, and storms enjoy no advocate like the seasoned waterfowler.

With low layers of scud advancing over the hills to the north, I can practically feel snowflakes coalescing in the gloom overhead. And then they're falling, if that's really the right word: lazy white petals coat my hat and Rocky's eyebrows and finally the whole dim landscape. Despite all I've said about the virtues of inclement weather, it's hard not to experience a chill above and beyond the simple fall of the thermometer. The front's arrival marks a real change of seasons: I've heard my last elk bugle and cast my last dry fly for the year. Because I love those things too, it's hard to avoid a note of sadness at their passage.

But nature, in contrast to certain Wall Street accounting firms, always keeps her books fairly. There will be compensation for everything autumn's first real storm has cost, provided we can endure long enough to receive. Trusting neither the weather report nor the calendar (a deliberate exercise in denial, no doubt) I'm dressed a bit lighter than I should be. But with less than an hour of light remaining and a warm Lab to lean against, I remain determined to see the afternoon through to its conclusion.

And suddenly the birds appear, circling over the cottonwoods to put the wind in their faces as they descend: prime northern mallards, orange-legged and stuffed with grain. Opening day doldrums forgotten, I rise to meet them, and when the shooting is done the chilly afternoon feels less like the end of one season than the beginning of another.

Foul is fair. Indeed.

Set up for divers on the Columbia.

CHAPTER TWENTY-SEVEN

Trophy Waterfowl

LORI AND I HADN'T SEEN THE SUN since we crawled up Lolo Pass into a blizzard on our way from Montana to Washington. Five days had passed since then, and the tenacious layer of ice fog hanging over the Columbia River showed no signs of dissipating. A relentless chill hung over the water, and the monochromatic landscape would have felt as oppressive as the weather had it not been for the long lines of divers trading up and down the river. I've always been amazed by the ease with which ducks in the air can compensate for lack of personal comfort.

Ready for a break from our steady diet of mallards on the creeks back home, I'd traveled to eastern Washington eager for something new. And I'd made no secret of one particular ambition: a drake canvasback for the taxidermist. Enjoyable as the waterfowling can be around our remote Montana home, we lack the big water that attracts divers and I hadn't even seen a can in my home county for years. But now canvasback numbers were doing so well in the Pacific Flyway that Washington's regulations allowed two per day for the first time in memory.

The abundant bluebills rocketing past our decoy spread provided me with an opportunity to review the differences between shooting mallards hanging over decoys and knocking down divers at twice my usual range. I won't deny that I missed a bird or two that I should have killed. But by the time a third bluebill completed my daily sub-quota of scaup, I'd found diver range again as a drake redhead quickly learned.

With one frigid hour of shooting light left, it was time to hunker down in the skiff and wait for the bird I'd come for all along.

I have mixed feelings about trophy hunting, a process I prefer to call selective hunting to diminish the emphasis on measuring what's been shot. I sometimes enjoy the challenge of holding out for an exceptional animal when I'm hunting big game with my bow. But I also feel that modern hunters concentrate too often on horns and antlers at the expense of what really counts: knowledge of wildlife, experience in the field, and meat for the table, to cite a few examples.

At its best though, selective hunting has its place. It generally takes more skill to hunt selectively than to settle for whatever comes along, and skill development is one of the most rewarding aspects of the hunting experience. My own enthusiasm for selective big game hunting derives largely from the additional time selectivity allows me to spend in the field each season. Even though I limit myself to hunting big game with traditional bows, I'd fill most of my tags in short order if I didn't make the process even harder. Selectivity means more days spent outdoors, getting in shape, observing wildlife, and avoiding the unwelcome busyness of life in the modern world as long as possible.

These considerations may seem peripheral to the waterfowl hunter who customarily measures successful hunts by the pace of the shooting, the quality of the dog work, or the colors of the sunrise. Perhaps it should stay that way. However, there are circumstances in which the best elements of selective hunting translate nicely to the duck blind.

Duck hunters were among the first to exercise the principle of voluntary restraint. Initially driven by reduced limits during the drought years, waterfowl hunters learned to derive more satisfaction from fewer birds, a lesson that has carried over into times of abundance. The folks I hunt with recognize that regulations allowing hunters two hen mallards per day don't necessarily mean you should shoot two hens even if the opportunity arises. Nowadays, most serious duck hunters I know avoid shooting hens even if that means going home a bird or two shy of a limit. Three greenheads on the duck strap at the end of the morning registers more "trophy" value to them than the same three birds plus a pair of hens.

Selective waterfowling is about raising the bar as well as holding your fire. A few seasons back, as recalled earlier, I spent several days bobbing around the frigid seas off Kodiak Island trying to shoot an eider. Calm weather in the Gulf of Alaska kept the birds offshore and I never even saw one. Last year, I spent two mornings trying to ambush a flock of cranes visiting a barley field. Nothing came of that effort either, but in both cases the decision to concentrate on something difficult rather than falling back upon the same old routine created a wealth of memories and made me a better waterfowl hunter.

Back on the Columbia, Lori, Michael, and I continued to watch birds come and go: bluebills, redheads, goldeneyes... everything except the long-necked silhouette I wanted to see. I still had some room in my limit and some of the shots looked tempting, but I had become a hunter on a mission.

"Drake can!" Michael whispered suddenly from the stern.

"I think it's a redhead," I replied when I picked the bird up in the distance.

"No it's not!" Michael insisted. "It's..."

By then the duck had turned broadside in its first circuit about the decoys and I could see that Michael was right. Fighting the first case of buck fever I'd experienced in years, I let the single circle us twice more before concluding that this was as good as it was going to get. Then I rose, drove the barrel of the shotgun farther out in front of the bird than I ever imagined possible, and slapped the trigger. Time stood still as the shot column stretched out across the water. The bird's collapse seemed like a miracle.

"We've still got room for a few more birds," Michael pointed out once we'd collected the can.

"I'm happy to stay if you want to," I replied as I unloaded my gun. "But I'm done for the day." And why not? I had the trophy I'd come for.

Opening day on a quiet Montana slough.

CHAPTER TWENTY-EIGHT

The Start of It All

NOWADAYS I LIVE in semi-arid country on the cusp between the Central and Pacific Flyways. While our late season shooting on spring-fed creeks can be spectacular, I have to travel to enjoy big wetlands and early season waterfowling, when autumn colors are at their best and snow and ice have yet to dominate the landscape. I do so regularly, to venues as diverse as coastal Alaska and the Alberta prairies. While this arrangement affords me plenty of duck hunting, I miss the traditions of opening day at home.

This year I decided to so something about it. A couple we knew socially reported large numbers of ducks on the pond near their country home. Newcomers to the area, neither of them had done any hunting before, but both were enthusiastic about the idea. I scouted the pond the day before the opener and set up a makeshift blind. While Lori rounded up appropriate clothing for our friends that night, I gathered gear and watched Rocky dance around the house in a frenzy. Suddenly I remembered how much the anticipation of opening day reminds me of a childhood Christmas Eve.

Opening days and I go back a long time. I was a toddler when I experienced my first, as recounted in a later chapter, and I've never forgotten that experience. I also remember the first opener I almost missed. I was serving my medical internship in Montreal when I realized that the emergency room schedule would keep me out of the field on opening day. Somehow I conned a colleague into covering for me, and by sunrise I was banging down mallards in a Quebecois farmer's cornfield. I barely had time to scrub off the dirt and feathers before reporting for duty again that afternoon.

My next near miss took place in Alaska years later. While the September waterfowl opener was nearly sacrosanct in our circle, we'd planned a long wilderness float trip for caribou and rainbow trout that year, and when the waterfowl opener rolled around we were still out in the Bush without a shotgun among us. I'd just realized what day it was when I spotted a flock of teal in a backwater. After beaching the raft, I made a careful stalk with my longbow and managed to kill one. One teal split four ways over an open fire may not be much of a duck dinner, but it kept a Ripkenesque string of opening days alive.

In fact, the delightful craziness of opening day is a worldwide phenomenon. For pomp and circumstance nothing can rival the Glorious Twelfth in the British Isles, although the red grouse, the object of all that attention, is nothing fancier than the willow ptarmigan I've killed by the score in Alaska while "rough shooting". As for waterfowl, no one does opening day quite like the Kiwis. As a friend from New Zealand once explained: "Don't try to get anything done here on the first Saturday in May… unless it involves duck hunting."

Every opening day is an event, but nothing adds to the anticipation like hard work beforehand. Back when I lived in the remote northeastern corner of Montana, we didn't have much to do late in the summer except catch catfish and prepare for duck season. Every night after work, my two regular hunting partners and I would set off to scout the local potholes and build blinds. Those were wet, wonderful years on the prairie and our reward for all that sweaty labor came reliably on the first weekend every October. The local wetlands produced incredible numbers of ducks then, and I've never enjoyed better opening day shooting. The limits of blue-wings and pintails were gratifying enough, but the real satisfaction derived from the pre-season effort as much as the shooting.

What ended my personal streak of consecutive opening days? It's tempting to round up the usual suspects: competing outdoor interests, crowded schedules, and (shudder) advancing age. Truth is, I no longer live in an area where the opening day of duck season has a lot to offer... or so I thought. This year, the sense of something missing just wouldn't go away as duck season rolled around. My sense of loss had nothing to do with shooting; there would be plenty of that later. It was about dogs, friends, and the childlike inability to fall asleep the night before something important is going to happen. It was about opening day, and I missed it.

So there we were at 6 o'clock the following morning, gulping coffee before the hike down to the pond. Since I'd decided to let our host and hostess do the shooting, I didn't even carry a gun. As the horizon dipped slowly toward the rising sun, the conversation inside the blind reminded me that most of what I'd learned about ducks in 50 years wasn't as obvious to novices as it was to me. Our friends asked more questions than I could have imagined, but sharing knowledge born of experience seemed more important than shooting. I never regretted the decision to leave my own gun behind.

Studying my watch, I counted down aloud to legal shooting light. At the precise moment they became fair game, a pair of mallards appeared over the decoys. "Take the drake!" I cried. To Rocky's obvious dismay, no one did. Those were the only birds we saw all morning.

No matter. Two quiet hours in a duck blind had just reminded me what really matters on opening day: sunrises, dogs, and good company, with duck dinners purely optional.

Blue-winged teal.

CHAPTER TWENTY-NINE

The Best Laid Plans

IT WAS ONE OF THOSE GOLDEN Indian summer days on the high plains whose memory only improves over time. Our legs were young then and we had permission to hunt virtually anywhere we wanted, so Dick LeBlond, Ray Stalmaster and I had spent a long morning running down a typical eastern Montana mixed bag of sharptails, Huns, and sage hens. As I recall, we even had an antelope buck in the back of the rig as we headed toward home.

Elaborate dinner plans awaited us. We had a few of everything but not a lot of anything (except for the antelope, which really needed to hang for a few days), so we'd decided to treat our families to a mixed grill from the prairie. The more variety the merrier when it comes to that kind of culinary adventure, which explains our excitement when we saw the flock of teal resting on a little stock pond.

A quick look at the terrain confirmed that a legitimate sneak was impossible. A hundred yards of water lay backed up behind the old earthen dam spanning the coulee, and the birds were on the opposite end of the pond surrounded by nothing but level ground and scrubby sage.

"We need a sacrificial lamb," I theorized. "Two of us can sneak up the coulee and get behind the dam while the third swings around through the sage and flushes the birds. With luck, they'll fly right over the dam and we can add blue-wings to the menu."

"You guys take the dam," Ray volunteered graciously before I could say rock-paper-scissors.

"Give us 15 minutes to get into position," I said, and then Dick and I set off for the coulee with Sky at heel.

We made deadline, barely. As Dick and I began to inch our way up the backside of the dam, Sky's soft whine made it clear that he really wanted to bust over the top and ruin everything, but he was too experienced to yield to temptation. When I finally poked my nose through the dry grass on top I could already see Ray sauntering toward the ducks, and then they were airborne.

"Get ready!" I hissed to Dick... unnecessarily as it turned out, for the teal had other ideas. Just beyond shotgun range, they executed a tight midair turn and headed back toward the opposite end of the pond, where they flew right over Ray's head. Dick and I could only stare in disbelief as our plainly visible sacrificial lamb executed a nice double.

Soon the three of us stood side by side at the waterline while I unloaded my shotgun to send Sky on the first retrieve. Dick had just purchased a new double which neither Ray nor I had enjoyed an opportunity to study before.

"Let me take a look at that new gun of yours," Ray suggested casually as we watched Sky churn back toward shore with the first teal in his mouth. Just as Dick and Ray swapped shotguns, I heard the whistle of wings somewhere overhead. As only teal will do, the flock of blue-wings had decided that three men and a Lab in plain sight weren't going to keep them off their pond. As they barreled in for a low pass, Ray threw up Dick's new shotgun, the only loaded weapon among us, and smoothly doubled again.

"I like it," he opined casually in the stunned silence that followed his second shot. "Shoulders naturally, great balance..."

"We want a new sacrificial lamb!" I bellowed in protest, and then all three of us dissolved in laughter.

[126]

More than any other wing-shooting endeavor, the pursuit of waterfowl is a game of strategy. From the most elaborate goose spreads to stock pond jump-shooting excursions, we spend far more time planning to shoot than actually shooting, and therein lies much of the joy of the undertaking. Usually, the bag at the end of the day bears at least some resemblance to the accuracy of the planning. But not always, for as Burns once warned, "The best laid plans of mice and men…"

Personally, I welcome a little chaos when I'm hunting ducks. Unpredictability is just one important way in which nature expresses the capacity to mystify and amaze. If everything went according to plan, autumns wouldn't be nearly so interesting. Not to suggest that I'm jumping for joy when the geese decide to feed in a field two miles away from our spread, but I've learned to live with such developments.

After all, the four teal we added to the pot those many years ago were just duck soup in the end. But the look on Dick's face when he realized he'd handed off his loaded shotgun at the critical moment?

Priceless!

Late season on a spring fed slough.

CHAPTER THIRTY

Late Season

I DIDN'T HAVE THE HEART to look at the thermometer when we left home in the dark this morning, but this isn't the kind of cold that requires a number to describe its authority. The amplified acoustics, layers of structural icing on the foliage along the creek, and impossible brilliance of the winter constellations overhead combine to define the setting better than a column of mercury ever could. Let's just agree that it's too cold for rational people to be outdoors, and let it go at that.

It's also too cold for water to last long in its liquid state, and since water defines habitat for ducks this would seem an unlikely time to be hunting them. Credit the unique hydrology of the little spring creek for the resolution of this paradox. One of many similar natural marvels hidden in the landscape surrounding our home on the high plains, this one rises by magic from a damp spot in the ground and wanders across a half mile of willow studded bottomland before joining a nearby river that has been locked under layers of ice for over a month. But issuing from the ground at a constant temperature the creek itself never freezes, and somewhere out there in the vanishing darkness are flocks of mallards that know all about it.

This is the final week of what has already been a generous

waterfowl season, and we really don't have to be here. In fact, when the alarm clock sounded earlier Lori—admittedly a fair weather duck hunter—made a halfhearted plea to sleep in, but the Labs and I outvoted her. (I've never encountered weather conditions unpleasant enough to quell an experienced retriever's enthusiasm for duck hunting and hate to imagine them.) As I start to pitch the blocks onto the creek's inky surface, I congratulate myself for our resolution. By this time next week rising early to go duck hunting will no longer be an option, and that fact alone may be enough to explain my long affinity for the late season.

The waterfowling literature is full of opening days, with good reason. That's when the weather is pleasant and the birds most likely to decoy readily, and the inherent sense of anticipation leading up to opening morning is as close as most of us will ever come again to the excitement of a childhood countdown to Christmas. But in my own contrary way I've always been partial to the opener's mirror image on the calendar: the waning days of the season, when the birds are as educated as they'll ever be and the casual hunters have oiled their shotguns down and put them back in the cabinet for the year. No time for the faint of heart, the late season has plenty to teach us, about ducks and duck hunting and sometimes about ourselves.

Even as a kid too young to carry my own gun, duck hunting fascinated me right to the bitter end. I spent my childhood in upstate New York, where a brace of woodies was a big deal, a black duck a trophy. I can still remember lobbying hard for a duck hunt instead of a run through some local grouse cover one bitter November morning back then. It fell to my endlessly patient father to point out that the pond that held our duck blind was frozen solid.

Nothing taught me appreciation of the seasons' passage like duck hunting during my years in Alaska. Opening mornings on Cook Inlet tidal flats often found us jump-shooting teal in shirtsleeves. A week or so later the ponds would be black with ducks as interior lakes to the north began to freeze, and by the end of the month it would all be over. I soon learned to feel the grip of winter approaching in every shot I fired and every retrieve the dog completed. It always turned out to be later than I thought—an obvious metaphor for life itself. At times the sense of helplessness in the face of nature's power to take away what had so recently been given felt overwhelming. I eventually solved that dilemma practically if not philosophically by scheduling regular hunting trips to Kodiak, where December storms drove sea ducks off the open sea and into the bays, and the late season lasted longer than I did.

Nowadays, a December road trip to visit my parents at the Barker Ranch—a DU habitat project in eastern Washington in which they've held a longstanding interest—has become a regular part of our late season agenda. That's not necessarily the surest time to hunt the place, since cold fronts can freeze the ponds and send the ducks off to the nearby Columbia. But after three straight months of shotguns, bows, and arrows close to home I'm always ready for that kind of family reunion. Besides, the variety there (the bag can include anything from wood ducks to divers) sets the stage perfectly for the final weeks of the season at home, where there is seldom an opportunity to shoot anything but mallards.

A problem my duck hunting friends in other places assure me they'd love to have, and one Lori, Kenai, Rocky, and I are about to face this morning… Sometimes a limit of late season spring creek greenheads means waiting patiently for birds to arrive as singles or in pairs, but today my intuition tells me we're in for something more dramatic, and sure enough. Just as the sun clears the horizon, a distant wave of feeding chuckles that can only come from a large flock of birds rises somewhere behind us. Young Kenai looks befuddled, but Rocky, the veteran, already has the inbound flock locked onto his radar screen. Finally, tightening vortices of birds are circling the blocks while I whisper a reminder of blind discipline to Kenai and begin visually segregating drakes from hens.

The long season is almost over, and I miss it already.

Sequim Bay: set up on the salt.

CHAPTER THIRTY-ONE

The Sea Around Us

SOME OF THE MOST CHALLENGING duck hunting I've ever enjoyed took place along the coastline of Alaska, where I lived during the 1980's and still maintain a second home. On the upper reaches of Cook Inlet, where two hunting partners and I maintained a primitive cabin on the tide flats, the birds were mostly a familiar assortment of dabblers: mallards and pintails, widgeon and teal. During visits to friends on Kodiak Island however, the bag usually included an assortment of sea ducks: Barrow's goldeneyes, scoters, harlequins, and long-tailed ducks (as they are now officially known). But it wasn't the contents of the game vest at the end of the morning that defined the hunting; it was the proximity of the sea and all that the maritime ambience brought to bear upon the experience.

There was just no getting away from the brooding North Pacific. The smell of the sea filled the lungs, and the Inlet's 20-foot tides always stood ready to engulf the careless hunter. On clear fall days, the flight across the Inlet to the cabin could be spectacular, with Sky panting down my neck from the back seat of the airplane, the snowy peaks of the Alaska Range towering ahead of us, and white beluga whales frolicking beneath the wings. But even on the beautiful days it was impossible to forget that an engine failure over the Inlet meant a death sentence. Every landing on the little patch of high ground next to the cabin required careful study from the air to ensure that the last high tide hadn't left a log lurking in the grass. At night when the wind howled across the flats, the roar of the gusts made it impossible to forget that nothing stood between the cabin's occupants and hypothermia but a few sheets of plywood.

All of which only served to make the hunting more memorable. There were days when sudden ice on the distant Interior's lakes and rivers turned the tidal sloughs black with migrating ducks, and there were days when we were lucky if we could jump-shoot a few snipe as we hiked back to the cabin hoping that the tracks underfoot were left by brown bears with no particular ax to grind that night. Some days on Kodiak the sea ducks flew in such numbers that we were ready to pick up the blocks and go halibut fishing by the time the anemic sun crested the southern horizon. On other mornings, we simply sat there and froze. It scarcely matters now, for what I remember best isn't the sight of a goldeneye tumbling into the surf or Sky battling the current to make a retrieve. What I remember is the presence of the sea around us.

Too many of us from the heartland will never know the special pleasure of hunting ducks along the coast, and that's a shame. Salt water runs deep in the bloodlines of American waterfowling. Both the Labrador and Chesapeake can trace their origins back to the North Atlantic. The decoy carver's art and the basic form of many modern duck hunting techniques evolved there as well. The coast exposes the hunter to a variety of waterfowl seldom seen inland. And big water means big challenges; those who enjoy investing effort in their duck hunting will never find a better place to play.

My Alaska experiences notwithstanding, the notion that all saltwater duck hunting means battling the elements under arctic survival conditions doesn't hold up, as regular winter visits to friends on the Texas Gulf Coast have taught me. On one such recent trip, I found myself shucking layers of clothing on the walk from the house to the airboat dock, and I would have been all the way down to shirtsleeves save for the need for camouflage in the blind. I even got to swat a few mosquitoes, in January no less! Primed by the memory of an alligator lying under the dock the previous afternoon, I expressed my concerns about the dogs' safety. "Don't worry," our host assured me. "When it gets cold like this the gators lie dormant." Cold? All perceptions are indeed relative.

By the time we'd finished pitching the blocks into the brackish water surrounding the blind, enough birds had buzzed by through the gloom to assure me that the local five-duck limit would be over too soon if we let it. Lori and I took our time loading our shotguns as the sun rose sluggishly through the fog layer. I wanted to savor the setting without interruption as long as possible. The Port Aransas National Wildlife Refuge lay across San Antonio Bay to the south. The winter home to most of the continent's surviving population of whooping cranes, the refuge stands as a testimonial to what determined conservationists can do for wildlife. Of course, the ducks overhead did too.

By the time I finally chambered a pair of shells, I'd recognized the source of the *déjà vu* that had been haunting me all morning. Drop the temperature 40 degrees and trade ibises for sandhill cranes and alligators for brown bears, and I could have been back on the Cook Inlet flats. While the gentle tides of San Antonio Bay hardly compare to the Inlet's raging currents, the intertidal zone shares common characteristics at any latitude: fertility, biodiversity, the pervasive saline smell of the sea.

The bag hanging from my game strap at morning's end reflected that diversity. In addition to teal, bluebills, and mallards, Lori had killed a beautiful drake pintail and I'd dropped a canvasback. In its own way, that lone can represented a biological success story as significant as the whooping cranes across the bay. It was hard to believe we would be headed back to the frozen plains the following day.

Our principal home state of Montana has everything an outdoorsman could ask for except an ocean. That's why I never ignore an excuse to visit one, especially during duck season.

Don and Kenai at their favorite slough.

CHAPTER THIRTY-TWO

The Slough

CHINOOK WINDS are a regional phenomenon here on the east slope of the Rockies: great blasts of warm air that spill over the mountains from the southwest during the winter, melting snow and ice like a giant hair dryer. I knew they were coming that day, and I wanted to get in one last shoot on my favorite spring-fed slough before every frozen pond in the county opened up and the mallards dispersed in all directions.

Gusting winds had whipped the water's surface to a froth by the time Lori and I arrived in the dark. After pitching a dozen blocks into the gloom, I realized that the decoys with the smaller keels had immediately turned over in the gale. With my feet feeling their way along for the seam of gravel that marks the old streambed, I somehow managed to retrieve them without bogging down in the mud. Then there was nothing to do but hunker down in the willows with Rocky, turn our backs to the wind, and wait for shooting light.

Sunrise wasn't much that morning by prairie standards—just a dull, gray glow fighting its way through layers of clouds scooting along before the wind like runaway horses. Fortunately, we didn't have to depend on scenic ambience to reward us for enduring the alarm clock's early blare. Five minutes after my watch officially made us duck hunters,

Rocky's face turned upward and there was the first flight of birds.

Their ground speed on the downwind leg of their approach made them look more like F-16's than mallards, but they paid for the free ride the moment they turned into the wind. They appeared to be struggling just to make it back to the water, but then they were hanging above the decoys with their orange feet extended. I whispered for Lori to "Take 'em!" and she did.

I didn't even raise my shotgun. I told myself I wanted to concentrate on working the dog, but the truth was I knew we were in for a magical morning and I didn't want it to end too quickly.

According to my dictionary, a slough is "an area of soft, muddy ground; a swamp or swamp-like region." Not everyone accords them as much esteem as duck hunters. In The Pilgrim's Progress, John Bunyan's stalwart protagonist sinks in one under the weight of his unredeemed sins. The image proved so durable that his Slough of Despond reappeared in subsequent works by Hawthorne, Bronte, and Forester. I suppose it's all a matter of perception.

In fact, sloughs are small biological marvels, especially in dry terrain like the Montana prairie, where a half-acre of muddy water can foster biodiversity out of all proportion to its size. A prairie slough may not look like much to an observer accustomed to big water, but in the land of the blind the one-eyed man is king.

My favorite slough is just a wisp of clear water lying a quarter mile off an equally diminutive "river" that really should be called a creek. But it supports a dense growth of reeds and willows, and in contrast to the stock ponds that dot the surrounding ranchlands, the slough, fed by a warm subterranean aquifer, never freezes. By the time the thermometer plummets and the big flights of mallards arrive from Alberta (every banded bird I've killed there began life north of the border), it's one of a limited number of open water options left. That description might make hunting the ducks that use it sound like shooting proverbial fish in a barrel, but the valley supports dozens more spring-fed bodies of water, so decoys, calling, and good technique are always part of the game.

The slough has always meant more to me than duck hunting. The surrounding terrain is good upland bird habitat. I take a limit or two of roosters there every season, and I've pass-shot enough sharptails incidentally from my blind to prove that steel shot will kill grouse as well as waterfowl. The slough is also home to muskrats, marsh hawks, and mink; keening killdeer, nattering yellowlegs, and all the other forms of wildlife that make the "barren" prairie come alive for those willing to stop, look, and listen. The satisfaction of knowing the wildlife is there cannot be expressed as limits of ducks even though there have been plenty of them.

The land belongs to a long established ranch family, old friends from my three decades as a local physician. If anything about the slough means as much to me as the wildlife, it's the hospitality. I sometimes think of it possessively, but only because I care about the memories it has produced and the wildlife it supports. For all these years, that's been good enough for me.

I was glad I'd decided to hold my fire and work the dog that morning. Despite the six busy seasons under his collar Rocky quickly started acting like a puppy, with good reason. Waves of mallards had stacked up down the valley on approach to the slough, and the birds in the air were distracting him from the two pair Lori had soon dropped in the brush and reeds across the water. A little face time soon settled him down however, and once he had the fourth drake lying beside us in the willows I decided to stand and take the next set right beside my wife.

Full disclosure: although they should be easy, birds hanging over decoys in a high wind sometimes cause me problems because of my fast shooting style, and I missed the back half of what should have been a slam dunk double. I felt less startled by the miss than by how little I cared. By the time Rocky had delivered two more drakes, it was already time to reload and concentrate on the next set. The slough was treating us to something special that morning, and for once I was smart enough to know it.

Rocky with a pintail drake.

CHAPTER THIRTY-THREE

Just Say Maybe

FLYING AS ONE, the little flock started its descent from an improbable height. "No way," I'd muttered the moment I followed Rocky's gaze skyward and spotted them high above the blind. But then they entered a precision turn suggesting interest in our decoys, cupped their wings, and began to plummet. The sound of the crisp October air whistling through their primaries spilled across the marsh, and I felt a shudder beside me on the bench, although I couldn't tell whether it arose from Lori or the dog. Just as I began to time my rise, all six birds seemed to bounce off an invisible shield overhead and then they were out of range again before I had a chance to react. Their climb appeared to involve no more effort than their approach, as if the whole maneuver had been conducted under zero gravity conditions. The net effect felt magical. and I relaxed my grip on the gunstock absent any regret for the shot I'd never fired.

"Pintails," I whispered wistfully, just as a certain citizen had once whispered "Rosebud".

"How could you tell what they were?" Lori asked. Her question brought me back to ground level as I watched the flock disappear into the distance. But as I started to offer a didactic reply involving slender profiles, arched necks, and the outline of the drakes' tail feathers silhouetted against the sunrise, I realized that these conventional field marks were all irrelevant.

"By the way they fly," I finally replied, an explanation that evidently required elaboration. I did my best, and the discussion that followed quickly evoked decades' worth of experience with one of my favorite waterfowl.

I began to hunt pintails seriously in the early 1970's. Those were lush years on the high plains, and ducks proved abundant around my new Montana home, none more so than pintails. I quickly developed a fascination with their command of the air and virtuosity in flight, traits unmatched among all other dabblers. On countless prairie mornings I watched in fascination as pintails circled the decoys, dropped their flaps, and flirted with a commitment to land. As delightful on the table as they were graceful on the wing, they became an obsession, and I started to hunt them selectively.

Those were the days of the point system in the Central Flyway, and with a dime price tag to count against the 100-point daily limit, sprig were what any stock analyst would have to call significantly undervalued. Coming out of one of those lonely marshes with ten pintails hanging from my duck strap became a regular goal even if that meant passing up seductive shots at mallards. With skies full of ducks and virtually no other waterfowlers in that remote corner of the plains, I was smart enough to realize that I was living the good old days.

But dry years followed the wet ones. Duck numbers declined, and because of their preference for nesting in marginal wetlands, pintails suffered more than most. The point system disappeared and the daily limit of pintails fell. Not that limits mattered; I spent enough time in the field to recognize what was happening, and I simply stopped shooting them. While I could justify my enthusiasm during times of plenty, those heady circumstances no longer applied. Besides, I was maturing as an outdoorsman. The species that had once taught me so much about the magic of waterfowl on the wing became an object lesson in an even more important principle: voluntary restraint.

By the time that little flock buzzed our decoys last season, I hadn't killed a pintail in years. During their first pass my thumb had found its way to the safety more or less by instinct, but when I spotted the birds returning for a second look I felt myself mired in conflict. Although pintail numbers were still down in comparison to historic records, I'd noted more of them than usual on local waters over the course the summer. And I could name several good reasons to stand and shoot a modern limit of two if they circled back in range: a young Lab in need of work, an opportunity to show one to Lori (who hadn't been with me during those glory years in the middle of nowhere), a sudden craving for a roast pintail dinner. But they did, and I didn't.

Right or wrong? Responsible or over-sentimental? None can truly say, but I've learned over the years that if I really have to ask myself whether I should or shouldn't in the field, the right answer is almost always no.

The time for me to shoot my next limit of pintails will come. Like great art, I'll know it when I see it. In the meantime, there's no limit on appreciation, self-imposed or otherwise.

Set up on a Washington marsh.

Section III

In the Field: Geese and Beyond

Wilson's snipe.

In the Field: Geese and Beyond

THROUGHOUT THIS COLLECTION, I've used the slightly awkward term "waterfowler" in numerous instances when the more conventional "duck hunter" would have done as well... almost. The choice is deliberate. First, the term evokes a sense of American history dating back at least as far as William Cullen Bryant's poetry. Second, it enforces the idea that the subject under discussion involves more than killing birds... or at least trying to kill them. Most important, it emphasizes that those birds do not necessarily need to be ducks.

Granted, most of us begin our waterfowl field careers hunting ducks, for obvious reasons: they're plentiful and can be taken successfully with unsophisticated strategies and a minimum of equipment (although that state of blissful, low cost naivety seldom lasts long among the truly stricken). And many of us hunt waterfowl for decades without paying much attention to anything else. But since variety really is the spice of life, it's easy to understand why so many of us eventually move on to sample different items from the menu.

Save for wild turkeys, geese are as close to big game as you can get while hunting a quarry that wears feathers. The qualitative distinction between hunting ducks and hunting geese derives from more than the difference in the size of the birds (which may not be that great, as you'll appreciate the first time you heft a plump mallard and a cackling Canada goose side by side). It's the size of the production that counts. Because of their habits and habitat preferences, geese are seldom taken casually.

Finally, there are the real oddballs of the waterfowler's world: the webless migratory game birds. Biologically related to ducks and geese little more than to woodpeckers, snipe and cranes owe their consideration here to two primary factors: they migrate and inhabit wetlands (both are also good to eat, fun to hunt, and enjoy recognition as migratory game birds by the ultimate arbiter, the Fish and Wildlife Service). Granted, I know seasoned hunters who regard them as little more than curiosities and openly dispute their status as "waterfowl". But I have come to explore possibilities, not to argue them.

So let us move on together to the next phase of the waterfowling experience: geese and beyond.

Cackling goose, formerly a subspecies of the Canada.

Migrating snows.

CHAPTER THIRTY-FOUR

O, Canada!

BY THE TIME THE ICE FOG begins to build over central Alberta early in November, the landscape looks like an image projected from an old black and white television set, and the fauna blend right in. The brightly colored birds have all followed the sun south, and what remains behind seems perfectly suited to the monochromatic winter months ahead: black-capped chickadees, white-breasted nuthatches, downy woodpeckers and, best of all, the last of the gray geese.

John Schneider and I had spotted them in the air the previous afternoon and followed them by truck like storm chasers on the heels of a tornado. Oddly silent beyond the invisible windshield, the undulating lines of geese eventually converged on a hundred-acre pea field that barely seemed large enough to hold the flocks milling overhead. A white frame farmhouse stood nearby, nestled neatly behind a well-kept shelterbelt. Although John hails from the area, he didn't know the farmer. "Never hurts to ask," I pointed out. Ten minutes later, we'd enjoyed a warm handshake, some jawing about the weather, and an invitation to return the following day with our shotguns.

Setting up in a nearly barren field always makes me feel exposed and obvious, especially when the birds have already proven their ability to survive a long season's worth of deception. But we knew how badly the geese wanted to return, and that realization sustained us as we set out the decoys and nestled the coffin-blinds into the lowest ground we could find. Finally there was nothing left to do but settle down against the frozen dirt and let our watch hands creep toward the appointed hour.

As usual when the air lies still and cold and geese are the quarry, I heard the birds before I saw them. The first distant bleat might have come from a barnyard dog, but the chorus built rapidly toward an unmistakable crescendo. Then I saw the flock silhouetted against the late afternoon sun, inbound and descending. John and I tried our best to ruin everything (You call it! No, YOU call it!), and we nearly succeeded. The wary birds were already flaring skyward by the time we finally acknowledged that one pass was all we would get and fumbled our way into shooting position. I mentally isolated one bird from the flock and slapped the trigger just as I reached the physical limits of my swing. The recoil's awkward vector punched me backward into the ground, but I retained the mental image of the bird crumpling at the sound of the shotgun's report. I didn't worry about the second barrel.

Brant, John's enthusiastic yellow Lab, exploded from his blind like a demon and ran the bird down before we had a chance to turn and watch the retrieve. By the time we'd reviewed the chain of command (This time you call it! No, YOU call it!), more goose talk was rising from the west, and I could distinguish three different lines of birds headed toward us from the orange quadrant of the sky. Brant had already burrowed his way back into John's blind where he lay whining softly, a model of eager yet disciplined anticipation.

At least one of us looked ready for the next round.

I've heard a lot of criticism of our neighbors to the north on the part of American sportsmen, most precipitated by Canada's firearm entry permit requirements, which many on this side of the border consider onerous. While I have no enthusiasm for pointless regulation, I've taken a disinterested view in this argument for one simple reason:

it's their country, folks, and they can run it as they see fit. I prefer to save my indignation for our own politicians, who certainly deserve their share. When I headed north that year to bowhunt with my friends, the thought of leaving my shotgun behind sounded less like a principled political statement than an act of sacrilege.

For the record, I found two minutes of firearm-related paperwork waiting for me when I arrived in Edmonton, not the hour's worth some commentators had warned against. It took some time to clear customs anyway, but that's just because the agent wanted to talk. Less than two months had passed since the September 11 tragedy, and he really wanted to know how we Americans were doing. And this much came through loud and clear: as far as he was concerned, we were all in this together. That kind of genuine human concern can make up for a lot more than the time I spent filling out forms.

So can all those geese.

One appealing aspect of setting out goose decoys and blinds almost anywhere in Alberta's vast prairie is that one never knows for sure what kind of geese will visit the spread. Canadas, snows, and speckle-bellies are usually all possible, and more than once I've taken all three from the same blind in one morning. (Of course, more than once I haven't taken any of the three, but that's another story.)

North of the border, Canada geese, the most familiar of the triad to most of us, are universally known as grey geese rather than Canadas, which I've always found paradoxical. The species is officially called the Canada goose in every official reference I've ever consulted, and in Canada, of all places, one would expect them to be known as such. I suppose we could all just call them honkers and be done with it.

But I'm sticking with "Canada" purely out of respect... for the birds and the country.

Late season geese rise from the Missouri.

CHAPTER THIRTY-FIVE

Long Shots

THANKS TO A MILD NOVEMBER, the geese arrived late that year, and by Christmas I hadn't killed a single one despite several mornings spent shivering in empty fields surrounded by useless decoys. Then a friend called to report that the birds had flocked into the Missouri River in front of his home by the thousands, which sounded like an invitation to me even if that wasn't what he originally had in mind.

His house sits on a wedge of property that includes a high bluff the birds fly over when they leave the river to feed each morning. This stretch of river bottom lies a hundred miles from my own home, and absent other landowner contacts in the area, we elected to set up on the bluff and try to pass-shoot a goose dinner without benefit of decoys. The plan admittedly sounded a bit far-fetched until we left the sanctuary of our host's kitchen in the dark. The cacophony of gabbling from the river confirmed the presence of bird numbers sufficient to allow even the proverbial blind hog a chance of finding an acorn.

The geese took their time leaving the river that morning, not that anyone really cared. As the sun broke behind us, we stared out across a scenic valley that has changed remarkably little since Lewis and Clark passed through two centuries earlier. Finally, the goose-talk built to a crescendo and birds started to lift off the water.

Staggered conveniently, geese began to flow past. Birds anywhere other than straight overhead clearly looked too far, and even those that passed at a vertical angle offered shooting only at the limits of my range. Even in retrospect, I don't know whether the three of us were deferring to one another, carefully considering ranges, or struggling to avoid embarrassment, but for some time no one fired a shot.

A long career as a bowhunter has enforced the virtues of getting close to game, which, as a waterfowler, translates into a preference for shooting decoying birds. But after an hour on top of the bluff, not to mention more geese than I'd seen all season, I finally realized that 50 yards was as good as it was going to get, which led to a difficult ethical decision: were those shot opportunities reasonable, wishful thinking, or worse?

Long shots…the term, initially derived from the hunter's vocabulary, has grown to describe any attempt unlikely to succeed, whether the activity takes place on the playing field, racetrack, stock market, or voting booth. While long shots in those situations may well lead to humility, there is seldom any ethical prohibition against taking them, and Americans are famously enthusiastic about risking such attempts. But hunting is different, since long shots in the field place the quarry rather than the hunter at risk.

I've always taken a dim view of sky-busting, or shooting beyond one's effective range. The rub derives from determining that range, which depends on many variables, especially the skill of the shooter. While decades of experience have probably left me safely in the better-than-average category, I hadn't pass-shot geese in some time, and I realized that missing, or worse yet, crippling, birds at long range is actually far less excusable than whiffing outright at mallards hanging over decoys.

But finally, I identified an inbound flock that looked just right. With plenty of time to get my feet set, I reviewed the technicalities of my gun and loads, factors ordinarily consigned to instinct. Knowing what we were in for, I'd selected a full choke over/under acquired in a horse trade decades before that seldom leaves the gun cabinet nowadays. Realizing that the birds were going to pass well beyond the range at which steel shot begins to slow, I consciously made myself drive the muzzle a body-length farther forward than my internal computer told me to before I slapped the trigger. The bird folded midair and collapsed in a satisfying heap, and I gladly settled for the single.

I can't describe the shooting that followed as easy, but we dropped a lot more birds than we missed, enjoyed a comfortable rapport with the dogs, and left with exactly what we'd come for: the makings of a goose dinner adequate to feed not only ourselves but most of our friends.

All of which should tell us something. The rituals of waterfowling invite a continuing return to the familiar. But the world of ducks and geese remains vast and varied, as does its enjoyment. A fine line exists between respecting one's limitations and retreating from challenges. And the greatest satisfaction sometimes derives from hunting near the edge of the envelope… as long as it's done with due respect for the quarry.

Sunset over an Alberta grain field.

CHAPTER THIRTY-SIX

Serious Geese

THE FIRST FLIGHT APPEARED at a range measured in miles rather than yards, a wavy line silhouetted against the dull glow of the sunrise far away across the lonely Alberta prairie. The gabbling chorus identified the birds as a mixed flock of speckle-bellies and snows, the latter notoriously difficult to decoy. But they remained headed relentlessly in our direction, and anticipation began to warm the meager confines of our blinds. When the birds started to veer off to the north, we offered some backtalk with our calls and they changed course favorably in response. As they crossed the perimeter of the field, the lead birds cupped their wings and began their descent. Against substantial odds, our long, lonely work in the pre-dawn darkness had earned their attention. Hope yielded grudgingly to certainty. At best, we might enjoy several seconds of waterfowling excitement at its finest. At worst, we were guaranteed a ringside seat at one of nature's greatest spectacles.

I like to think I've outgrown buck fever, but there were the distinctive symptoms of that strange malady all over again: the sweaty palms, the pounding heart, the awestruck suspension of disbelief. A sense of *déjà vu* made me shiver, drawn not from decades of experience in duck blinds, but from memories of whitetail bucks lumbering down fence rows in my direction, of bull elk and moose succumbing to the improbable lure of my calls. And finally, as the specks at the leading edge of the flock dropped their flaps and slowed their airspeed to a tantalizing crawl, the morning's central realization:

This experience defied the usual definitions of waterfowling. I was hunting big game.

While I'm plenty serious about many elements of outdoor sport (downright fanatical, in fact, according to rational observers like my wife), I can't call myself a serious goose hunter. Credit or blame a combination of factors: a relative paucity of geese in my home county, a host of competing outdoor interests during goose season, and above all an ability to satisfy most of my passion for waterfowl with a handful of decoys, a good dog, and a few cooperative mallards. Most of the geese I kill each fall die more or less by accident. While I enjoy shooting those birds by serendipity (and enjoy eating them even more), I'm honest enough to acknowledge that I'm missing something.

Fortunately, I have friends who are serious goose hunters, and I manage to charm my way into invitations to accompany them several times each season. Despite the high mileage on my personal odometer, these expeditions always arouse a certain childish glee. I've always been a sucker for the Big Show, and rising in the dark to place decoy spreads measured in hundreds rather than dozens qualifies as such by any definition. Even when the big birds stand us up, the sheer magnitude of the production invariably leaves an aftertaste of accomplishment. And when geese actually appear on the horizon and begin to express interest in all of our elaborate stratagems… well, that's buck fever territory all over again, and I hope I never outgrow it.

The birds themselves certainly know how to play their assigned part. No matter what the species, geese on the wing make an impression qualitatively more compelling than other waterfowl, a distinction the size of the birds itself cannot explain. Sheer numbers contribute to this phenomenon, however irrationally. The bag isn't going to change whether the flock headed toward the decoys numbers in the dozens or the hundreds, but a raucous vortex of geese swirling overhead never fails to take my breath away. Simple challenge also contributes to goose hunting's allure. Geese are inherently wary birds, and sucking a flock into shotgun range should be grounds for satisfaction whatever the outcome of the actual shooting. While geese on the table draw mixed reviews, at their best they can be a gourmet delight. Speckle-bellies represent wild cuisine at its finest, snows are consistently underrated, and I'm always happy to chew my way through a few tough Canada geese in search of the occasional bird that melts in the mouth.

But in the end it's the scope of the production that renders serious goose hunting special: the long hours of scouting, the acres of decoys, the meticulous attention to the detail of the blinds, the coordination and teamwork when it actually comes time to shoot. I've cited Aldo Leopold on the subject already, but his advice bears repeating: the value of any trophy from the field depends not on its size but on the amount of effort expended in its pursuit. By that simple definition, geese, taken seriously, rank among the most rewarding quarries of all.

New Zealand paradise ducks.

CHAPTER THIRTY-SEVEN

Betwixt and Between

Framed against the spectacular background of New Zealand's Southern Alps, the lush pastures and neatly framed farmhouses seemed to belong to another, simpler time. Although nearly a decade would pass before Peter Jackson filmed his Lord of the Rings trilogy nearby, I understood his impulse as soon as I got wind of it, for I remembered the countryside where we'd shot the birds as just the kind of place hobbits might live.

Kiwis enjoy a strong hunting tradition expressed nowhere as vigorously as in the pursuit of waterfowl. The traditional early May opening of duck season functions as a de facto national holiday, and in many rural areas the pace of business, such as it is in admirably laid back New Zealand, grinds to a virtual standstill. While our trip that year involved a complex agenda, I wasn't about to leave until I'd borrowed a shotgun and sampled the waterfowling about as far from home as it's possible to get.

"Remember," our host Doug Sheldon advised as I chambered a pair of shells behind the earthen dam. "We've got to drop one bird on the flush." While I didn't completely understand his insistence, I practiced shouldering the unfamiliar shotgun and promised to do my best.

We crested the dam to a sudden rush of wings and for an instant I caught myself staring at the alien shapes climbing skyward. Remembering my sworn duty just in time, I isolated one trailing bird and dropped it in the middle of the ten-acre pond. Fortunately, I'd kept my reservations about Doug's dog, a bouncy little Springer named Jimmy, to myself. The spaniel swam down the fallen bird as neatly as any seasoned Lab, and moments later Lori and I were studying our first paradise duck.

Although the 14 representatives of the unique genus *Tadorna* enjoy a vast geographical distribution, they somehow managed to miss North America completely. What rotten luck for us. Shelducks migrate widely throughout Europe and Asia, and I've encountered them personally in Australia (the Burdekin duck) and Southern Africa (the South African shelduck) as well as New Zealand. In Patagonia, the distinction between duck and goose becomes more confused in the genus *Chloephaga*, or sheldgeese, which includes the ashy-headed goose. Most species are strikingly beautiful. A friend who specializes in avian taxidermy for museums and collectors around the world states he'd rather work on shelducks than any other family of birds.

Depending upon one's point of view, they are either the world's largest ducks or among the world's smallest geese, confirming, to my eye at least, how arbitrary some biologic classifications prove to be when subject to scrutiny. The specimen that Jimmy quickly delivered felt midway in heft between a mallard and a snow goose: a species truly betwixt and between. Uncharacteristically in the world of waterfowl, in which females usually dress in drab plumage for the sake of camouflage on the nest, hen paradise ducks bear more vivid markings than the drakes. With a head and neck that looked as if it had been dipped in white enamel, a rich auburn mottled thorax, and iridescent green wing specula, the bird I'd dropped immediately impressed me as one of the most striking waterfowl I'd ever seen. And as if to fix the moment forever, she wore a band on her right leg.

Doug wasted no time clarifying his insistence that we drop at least one bird on the rise. It turns out that paradise ducks decoy like moths to a flame, and with that single hen propped up on a stick atop the dam we soon began to draw in singles and pairs as birds from the original flock filtered back to their home water. Down to shirtsleeves in the sunshine, we sat in the grass, recently trimmed by one of the countryside's ubiquitous flocks of sheep, and told hunting stories until we heard the cry of inbound birds, at which point we crab-crawled into the one nearby clump of brush. I quickly came to terms with my borrowed gun, and the birds that fell provided ample opportunity for Jimmy to make me rethink my original dim opinion of his breed while Lori fussed with the camera. The measured pace of the shooting felt just right in a country that wisely refuses to hurry, and by the time we finally headed back to Doug's farm we were toting as many paradise ducks as we cared to shoot.

I'll admit my trepidation when Doug's charming wife Hillary informed us of her plans to breast the birds and grind them into duck burger, but once again I wisely kept my opinions to myself. Hillary proved to be a fine cook, and had I expressed my reservations earlier I would have had to eat my words right along with the finely seasoned duck loaf she placed on the table as the sun went down.

That trip to New Zealand involved, among other things, a week in the Southern Alps with my longbow in search of red stags and a quixotic attempt to show our plainly skeptical hosts that it is possible to catch king salmon on a fly. (The South Island of New Zealand is the only place in the world where transplanted kings have successfully established breeding populations outside the North Pacific.) But even after that excitement and adventure, it was my encounter with a gorgeous bird that can't decide whether it's a duck or a goose that left the most indelible impression of all.

That's why that first hen stands on our mantle now, mounted by my taxidermist friend with a passion for her kind, complete right down to the bracelet above her ankle.

Rocky with a mouthful of snipe.

CHAPTER THIRTY-EIGHT

A Bird in
the Hand

WITH THE SLATE JUST WIPED CLEAN by falling water bound for nearby Cook Inlet, the mud along the edges of the tidal guts contained more than enough fresh brown bear sign to keep me on my toes. Furthermore, Sky loved to slip from heel and go hunting whenever we were in the field, and his sudden insistence upon remaining glued to my side suggested that he could smell bogeymen hidden somewhere in the grass. Hence my brief sense of panic when the first snipe erupted underfoot with an explosion of wings that sounded several sizes too large for the bird.

Rattled by the flush, I took a moment longer than usual to mount my gun, track the darting target… and miss. But I settled down with my second barrel, which sent the snipe tumbling toward the grass in a satisfying puff of feathers. Brown bears or no, Sky wasn't about to pass up the opportunity for a retrieve. But when he returned to my side moments later, my first glance at his muzzle made me think he'd uncharacteristically failed in his mission.

A bit of study corrected that misimpression as I noted a long bill dangling from the corner of the dog's mouth like a comma. Moments later, the entire bird lay cradled in the palm of my hand where closing my fist effectively made it disappear (save once more for that incongruous bill). Had I really flown all the way across the Inlet to battle tides, weather, and bears for birds that would barely fill a teacup?

With the possible exception of the sandhill crane (which certainly represents the opposite end of the size spectrum), Wilson's snipe may be North America's most atypical waterfowling quarry. While some might argue against their very inclusion in this category, I defer to no less an authority than our federal government. They live near water, they migrate, and you need a duck stamp to shoot them legally. Q.E.D.

Over the years I've hunted snipe across a remarkable range of geography and habitat, from Arctic tundra to cactus-fringed pans in south Texas. Whether I've been dressed in layers of wool or shirtsleeves, I've always enjoyed hunting snipe, both because of their affinity for wild places and the challenge they offer on the wing. All who think they know shotguns deserve to spend a day trying to keep shot columns out in front of snipe as they dart across the grass or descend in crazy spirals toward a waterhole. They may be tiny, but they've provided comeuppance to better shots than me.

Despite all this, snipe have left some of their most vivid personal impressions when I'm not even carrying a shotgun, now that I do my turkey hunting with bow and arrow. Against the serene backdrop of a clear April sky, their aerial mating displays inevitably demand my ears' attention when my hearing is attuned to the possibility of a gobble somewhere in the distance. And when I finally spot the source of all that quavering racket silhouetted against the sunrise, the sound seems so big, the bird so small... just as that dead snipe did resting in my hand all those years ago in Alaska.

I once wrote a story about snipe hunting that generated an angry letter from an uninformed reader wondering how I could shoot shorebirds that I didn't plan to eat. Excuse me? Snipe are delicious; in fact, when properly prepared they rank among the best of all wild fowl. A late friend from Texas who could afford to eat whatever he wanted once spent two days encouraging me to shoot the snipe on his ranch just so we could eat them together for breakfast.

And why else had I bothered to fly a hundred pounds of Labrador retriever all the way across Cook Inlet?

Back on the tide flat, I chambered another load of #8's and forged ahead into the grass. By serendipity, the dog and I had arrived at the peak of the fall migration and the cover was full of snipe, interior birds that would be winging their way south at the first reminder of the hard northern winter following on their heels. Snipe flushed before the dog's eager nose, and I did my best. Some fell and others didn't. I learned to live with both results.

An hour later, the birds in the back of my game vest felt as if they weighed more than the shells remaining in its pockets, a measure of success that would barely withstand critical scrutiny. (Do the math.) But the afternoon had never been about a limit of snipe.

It had been about wilderness, adventure, and dog work, even if the results of a great shot could fit in the palm of my hand.

Eskimo turkey.

CHAPTER THIRTY-NINE

Eskimo Turkeys

SHIRTSLEEVE WEATHER during Alaska's duck season? It can happen, but a day's worth usually made me long for the familiar ambience of horizontal rain. Sweating miserably inside my waders, I cast the decoys into a shallow pool and settled into the grass beside the dog. Nothing stirred in the empty blue sky overhead, and absent any breeze, the blocks looked as listless as I felt. Panting rhythmically, even old Sky seemed unable to muster his usual enthusiasm. It wasn't long before I began to consider pulling up and flying north to explore the tail end of the silver salmon run in a favorite river nearby.

Suddenly, a series of ratcheting cries began to spill across the tide flat. The dog's ears rose in response as I scanned the sky for their source. The cranes already had their wings set by the time I spotted them low against the distant trees. Calculating their glide path like an outfielder judging a fly ball, I shifted into shooting position in anticipation of an unexpected opportunity. But no one deserves that kind of luck, and the flock of sandhills settled into the grass a hundred yards short. As their red-capped heads began to pivot alertly, I faced the moment of decision. More lingering beside a spread of decoys that looked as if they'd died last week, or a long, wet crawl toward the possibility of one of the North's most unlikely quarries?

When the going gets tough…

The 15 members of the avian family *Gruidae* enjoy a worldwide distribution that includes representatives on every continent but South America. Their regal bearing has been celebrated in Old World art for thousands of years. In the course of my travels I've spent hours observing brolgas in Australia and wattled cranes in Africa. Closer to home, the familiar story of the whooping crane's perilous decline and tentative recovery needs little introduction.

All of which admittedly makes it difficult to think about cranes as quarry, even the familiar and abundant sandhill. I saw plenty of the southern subspecies, the little brown crane, when I first moved to Montana. Hunting was by limited drawing permit only, and I never bothered to apply. In fact, I never considered hunting cranes until I moved to Alaska, where thriving populations of sandhills justified routine open seasons.

But abundance didn't necessarily translate into Thanksgiving dinners of Eskimo turkey, as I proved again that morning on Cook Inlet.

Ordinarily, the worst of the North's notorious mosquitoes (Alaska's real state bird) lie behind once waterfowl season gets underway, but not that day. Eager for one last round of torment before winter set in, bugs covered every exposed inch of my skin as I oozed through the mud toward the cranes. Years earlier I'd taught Sky to sneak along behind me on jump-shoots and the old guy was doing his best, but I was still worried about him. My concern wasn't for his discipline during the stalk but for his welfare after the shot, if one came. Friends had warned me about the damage a wounded crane's stiletto bill can inflict upon a dog, and I meant to take no chances. Our approach would end with a close, certain shot or none at all.

After an hour of the kind of maneuvering ordinarily reserved for Dall rams in the alpine, we were close but not close enough. Then I noticed a change in the rhythm of the birds' behavior as they probed the muck underfoot. Instead of one alert sentry, there were suddenly three, then six; the jig was up. The whole flock departed with a choreographed running start and their piercing alarm cries seemed to echo all the way to the Alaska Range and back. Covered with mud and bug bites, I rose slowly and watched them go, still uncertain whether I'd really meant to shoot one.

Full disclosure: of all the waterfowl discussed in this volume, the sandhill is the only species I've never killed. They're everywhere here on the high plains nowadays, and harvest restrictions have relaxed. I've even acquired a couple of crane decoys and a crane call. Maybe I'll get around to using them some day. Then again, maybe I won't.

In fact, my favorite memory of Alaska sandhills doesn't involve hunting them. My mind still wanders back to a crisp autumn day in the Interior when I was carrying a bow rather than a shotgun. I was glassing for moose when huge waves of migrating cranes suddenly appeared so far overhead that I probably wouldn't have noticed them save for their calls. For hours, I watched vast flocks circle above me in great, lazy spirals, as if they'd planned a private aerial ballet for my benefit. The overall effect proved hypnotic, and with soft, dry tundra underneath me I forgot about the moose in favor of the grand display high overhead.

Moral: there are many versions of the Big Show. Not all involve shotguns and dogs.

Snow on the wing.

CHAPTER FORTY

Goose Day

GOOSE DAY CAME EARLY THAT YEAR, thanks to a mass of cold arctic air that spilled down from the Alberta prairies during the last week of October. Unseasonable snow preceded the front, and we awoke one morning to an unexpected panorama of solid white. Then the temperature plummeted as the clouds lifted away, and by late afternoon the pond at the bottom of the hill had already frozen, sending the little flock of mallards that had frequented it all summer off to parts unknown. The following day, the sky was full of geese.

The snows came first, audible at distances almost too great for the human eye to perceive. But when I concentrated I could make them out, visible as nothing more than faint, undulating lines of pearly white as their beating wings flashed against the sun. Every flock seemed to be tracking the same southeasterly flight path at stratospheric altitude. No wonder I've never seen a snow goose on the ground in my home county.

By that afternoon the first of the Canadas had appeared, some as high and detached as the snows, others clearly looking for places to land. Oddly enough, I felt no immediate urge to break out the goose shells or track the birds to their local destinations while plotting the assembly of blinds and decoy spreads. As a matter of personal tradition, Goose Day is a phenomenon I choose to celebrate through observation alone. The rest can wait and so can I, confident that to all things there is indeed a season.

You won't find Goose Day noted on any calendar other than the one between my ears. Like all seasonal events that depend on nature rather than people for their timing, its arrival is difficult to predict. It usually takes place during the first week of November where I live, but you never know. Spawned by cold snaps a thousand miles away to the north, the geese often provide better weather forecasts than the weatherman. While nature can certainly confound, it never lies.

Recognizing Goose Day requires awareness of the natural world around us, and I'm always sadly amazed by the number of people who miss it completely. "Did you hear the snow geese pouring by last night?" I'll ask friends or colleagues at work, only to be greeted by blank looks of incomprehension. Over the years I've actually started phoning some of them and inviting them to step outside, look, and listen. They're the same friends I call when I can see the aurora borealis from my north-facing deck at night or a particularly spectacular moonrise crests the horizon, and by now they've all decided to humor me.

I enjoy a small but definite advantage over most folks in town when it comes to detecting the leading edge of this great annual migration. Goose Day usually coincides with the onset of the whitetail rut, when I spend a lot of time in the woods with my longbow being very quiet and attentive. More often than not I'll hear that first southbound flock of snows from a tree stand in the pines, and the 15 extra feet of elevation my perch provides puts me that much closer to the geese. Bowhunting from river bottom tree stands, I've had honkers sail past so close I could practically reach out and touch them. That too will come, when there's venison in the freezer and I'm more appropriately armed.

Since I truly enjoy hunting (and eating) geese, I'm always faintly surprised by my own passivity on Goose Day. Under ordinary circumstances I find it hard to watch a goose on the wing without reflexively timing my swing and feeling the heft of an imaginary shotgun against my shoulder. Such instincts come at a cost. Goose Day provides an opportunity to study my soon-to-be quarry unimpeded, and I seldom fail to notice things I might have missed while carrying a shotgun in my hand: the curve of an extended primary, the mysterious shuffling of leadership in the long V's passing overhead. Perhaps we all should declare these truces more often.

The great spectacle of Goose Day above all else represents a promise of things to come. The days on the calendar may flip past one methodical page at a time, but events outdoors never occur with such regimentation. The flow of natural cycles takes place in lurches and pauses, and nothing marks the abrupt transition of the seasons as definitively as waves of geese overhead. And the geese are just the beginning. Over the course of the next week, new flocks of plump northern mallards will appear on the creeks, bucks will breed does, and the last of the songbirds will disappear. I may well settle for a buck a bit smaller than the big one I've been watching all summer just so I can respond to the whining from the kennel by taking the Labs duck hunting. Change is literally in the air, and the dogs feel it as surely as I do.

Life at higher latitudes has its own rewards, a difficult concept to keep in mind when you've been snowbound for days and the pipes have started to freeze. But I've spent enough time in the tropics, where life outdoors never seems to vary much from day to day, to appreciate the pageantry of changing seasons. Nothing illustrates the cyclic pattern of nature's rhythms better than the migration of waterfowl. The birds that arrived here on the heels of that first cold front were someone's gift to us; when they depart they'll be our gift to someone else. And come next spring, a native Inuit hunter will look up into the sky, smile quietly to himself, and think: "Goose Day!"

Jimmy Buffet reminds us that it's always five o'clock somewhere. It's always Goose Day somewhere too, and as long as we guard our wild resources wisely, it always will be.

The moment of truth.

CHAPTER FORTY-ONE

Anticipation

FEW PLACES ON THE CONTINENT can feel as large and lonely as a remote corner of the Alberta prairie at dawn, especially on a crisp, clear morning like this. The perfectly circular horizon seems infinite, the freedom from human intrusion all but absolute. A few hundred miles to the north the province's burgeoning petroleum industry keeps giant machines rumbling around the clock, but from our perspective today all that human busyness might as well be taking place in another nation, or on another planet. There is nothing here today but the breeze and the stars overhead. And the geese.

They've been talking for over an hour now, a vast chorus of individual voices that distance and the sigh of the wind have blended into a steady, monotonous din. The volume of the racket has been increasing slowly ever since we finished setting out our vast decoy spread and settled in to listen and wait. Over the last 15 minutes the rate of increase in the sound level has accelerated wildly, like stock market prices in the days before the bubble burst, as the birds prepare to lift off at last from the distant reservoir. Finally. We hope.

For although waiting is a central element of many hunting experiences, few venues challenge the passage of time as sternly as lying supine in a frozen stubble field. The cold ground below extracts heat from the human body with relentless efficiency that the best outdoor clothing on the market cannot entirely resist. The coffin blinds we occupy seem all too aptly named; remaining motionless on your back in the cold and dark evokes an eerie suggestion of death itself. Fortunately, we have the swelling chorus from the distant reservoir to remind us otherwise.

And there is a method to the madness, for the trick is to make the huge, featureless sea of wheat stubble look exactly as it would if we weren't here, save for the decoys. This necessity derives from the remarkable ability of wild geese to detect danger with their eyes. As a bowhunter I've spent plenty of time operating close to almost every big game animal on the continent. As long as you know when to move (and more importantly, when not to) and don't do anything stupid, even the sharpest eyed of the lot—whitetails, pronghorns, wild sheep—often overlook you. But as every turkey hunter knows, birds are pattern recognizers. To a flock of wild geese, an anomalous lump in the middle of a field might as well be a beacon flashing a danger alert. Even lying quietly in our blinds hidden by natural windrows of straw, the best we can hope for is the ability to fool some of the geese, some of the time.

The idea of hunting waterfowl in the absence of water always strikes me as an oxymoron, which is one reason why I only set up in fields for geese once or twice each season. I miss the cast of characters that helps me pass the time between flights of ducks in swamps and sloughs, from muskrats and marsh hawks on the Montana prairies to ibises and alligators on the Texas Gulf Coast. In comparison, our surroundings today feel positively sterile. There just doesn't seem to be much of anything out here with us in our frozen field other than possibilities. And there's a differences between possibilities and promises.

That aura of uncertainty contributes to our sense of excitement in its own way. If we somehow knew that all this effort was going to produce furious shooting before the end of the morning, the whole undertaking would feel a lot less like a goose hunt and a lot more like a trip to the grocery store, and what fun is that? Sure we've scouted the field, but as the financial industry has recently reminded us, past performance is not a guarantee of future returns. For the geese, a hundred sections of stubble lie within commuting distance of the reservoir and even the truckload of decoys we set out in the dark can only make this one look so much more attractive than all the rest.

Suddenly the racket from the reservoir jumps up a notch in volume and changes pitch, suggesting a new level of confusion and excitement. The birds are off the water at last. Rocky has been at this long enough to know exactly what is going on, and I can feel him shift his weight and shiver with excitement in his nest of straw beside me. "Here they come!" our old friend Jeff Lander announces needlessly from my right as the first wave of airborne geese appears in silhouette against the distant sunrise. Just as unnecessarily, I pass this information along to Lori on my left before hissing one last demand for steadiness to the dog. Whatever random thoughts we might have entertained about rearranging the decoys or tweaking the appearance of the blinds blow away on the breeze. We lie committed to what we have already done.

Watching flights of geese approach your decoys is like watching an automobile accident from a street corner; events seem to take place a lot more slowly than they actually do. The first flock bypasses us to the north at altitude despite our calling, but even when they're still a mile away there's something different about the one that follows: a change in the cadence of their calls, a hesitation in the leaders' wing-beats. And then they've turned a few crucial degrees in our direction, cupped their wings, and started to descend.

Their agonizingly slow final approach provides an opportunity for all kinds of last minute anxiety. Did I ever actually remember to load my shotgun? Which one of us is supposed to make the final call when the birds reach shooting range? I know the answer to that one: Jeff.

"Take 'em!" he shouts, and the anticipation ends at last.

Busted! Gulf Coast snows.

CHAPTER FORTY-TWO

Chance of Snow

SINCE I'M ACCUSTOMED to enjoying prairie sunrises in silence, the din spilling over the hills to the east evoked an odd dissonance. That kind of busy auditory background usually arises from manmade sources like airports or freeways at rush hour, but we were many miles away from any such disturbance of the peace. The reservoir where the goose talk originated lay a good five miles away across the sea of stubble surrounding us, and as my brain extrapolated from the law of inverse squares by which sound waves disperse, I could scarcely imagine the noise level at ground zero. All this simply reminded me of an observation I'd first made decades earlier: Ten thousand geese preparing to take off from the water can make an unbelievable racket.

The slow crescendo taunted us as we lay shivering in our blinds, as if the birds were teasing us deliberately. Then the pitch of their chatter changed abruptly, and we could hear the sibilant sound of all those wings straining their way toward the cool, clear sky. In a matter of minutes we would know if our elaborate strategizing had accomplished its mission or come a cropper.

Finally we made first visual contact as lines of pearly white began to appear above the distant horizon. Win, lose, or draw, a serious snow goose hunt will almost always fulfill the promise of a spectacle, even if you never kill a bird.

I've lived tantalizingly close to good snow goose hunting all my life. When I was a kid growing up in western Washington snows would carpet the Skagit flats until the ground turned white every fall, but that was just a bit too far away to hunt casually, and I lacked the skills and knowledge to hunt wary geese effectively anyway. When I lived in Alaska, snows concentrated at the mouth of the nearby Kenai River by the thousands every spring on their way toward the Bering Sea, but during their southbound migration during hunting season they flew the hypotenuse of the triangle across the Gulf of Alaska toward their winter range and never came anywhere near my shotgun. Here in Montana, I've never killed a snow in my home county even though they stage in huge flocks at Freezeout Lake a hundred miles to the west. A regular hunting partner thought he had one day, but it fell to me to point out that he'd actually shot a far less common Ross's goose.

Since I've always had to travel for snow geese, I've never acquired the intimate knowledge of their pursuit that you pick up when you live with your quarry and hunt it regularly every season. But even though I can't pretend real expertise, those far-flung snow goose expeditions have produced some interesting encounters with the species.

March is always the grimmest month for outdoorsmen here on the high plains, so when the Fish and Wildlife Service first authorized spring snow goose hunting I received the news with glee. Montana doesn't have a spring season but North Dakota does, so a friend and I loaded my truck and set off eastward across long miles of melting snow until we saw geese overhead. We then spent two days lying in the mud while what looked like a million snows overflew us at high altitude. We never fired a shot.

The next spring, I headed south to Colorado to help a professional video producer film an ambitious subject: shooting snow geese with bow and arrow. Our set up was excellent, and by mid-morning I had emptied my quiver without cutting a feather, confirming my initial belief that the proper weapon to carry on a snow goose hunt is a 12-gauge shotgun. Although I've hunted big game exclusively with the bow for decades, I wound up trudging back to the truck for my double. I spent the rest of the day making the geese pay for the embarrassment I knew that earlier video segment would cause me.

One morning on the Texas Gulf Coast, a friend and I set up for ducks in our usual fashion. Thousands of snows winter in the nearby bay, but we felt content to settle for a morning of fast paced duck hunting and didn't even carry a goose decoy with us to the blind. Nonetheless, snows appeared low out of the fog all morning in singles and pairs, and by the time we picked up we had all the geese we could carry. The moral applies to virtually any kind of hunting even though it feels unjust after you've set out a hundred goose decoys: Being in the right place at the right time often matters more than all the preparation in the world.

The best snow goose hunting I've ever enjoyed has taken place on the Alberta prairie, right where this chapter began. Having a lot of birds around certainly helps, but the real difference is that I have friends there who care enough about goose hunting to do the work it takes to hunt snows the way you're supposed to hunt them. That's why we'd been lying in the dark at least an hour longer than necessary, surrounded by enough decoys to turn half the stubble field white. Snow goose hunting is always a gamble, and my Canadian friends believe that if you're going to do it at all, you ought to do it right.

As waves of geese began to draw closer, one flock veered in our direction, descending gradually while its leaders started to cup their wings. As I began to review the awkward mechanics of shooting from a coffin blind, I reminded myself not to expect anything easy. I've never had a snow goose actually try to land in my decoys, and pass shots at low flying birds with their wings set are the best I've learned to expect. Finally someone yelled, "Take 'em!" and we did.

Our chance had become a promise fulfilled after all.

Canada goose on the wing.

Section IV

Retrievers

Kodiak: Bob May's Chessies "retrieve" his skiff at the beginning of a hunt.

Retrievers

THE RELATIONSHIPS THAT DEVELOPED thousands of years ago between human hunters and the canids that eventually became their companions probably represent our own species' first attempt to domesticate wild animals. The marriage was evidently meant to last. While one can argue whether or not dogs are really man's best friends, they're almost certainly our oldest.

Nowhere is the value of this enduring symbiosis more apparent today than in the partnership between waterfowlers and their retrievers. While many modern dogs have devolved into lap-sitters and pot-lickers, the retrieving breeds remain true to their historical roots. In this context, service in the field reflects expression of inborn purpose rather than human exploitation. Working retrievers are happy because they're doing what they were meant to do. All of us should be so lucky.

The value of a good retriever derives first from practical consid-erations. Because of their habitat preferences, fallen waterfowl often land in places impossible to reach save by swimming, an unlikely option for human hunters in cold autumn weather. Even during dry-foot hunts over grain stubble, a keen nose can be essential in the pursuit of crippled birds. Trained retrievers solve these problems so efficiently that many experienced hands consider it unethical to hunt waterfowl without one. Count me in.

But even after the most spectacular retrieves, recovered birds only measure a fraction of the meaning retrievers bring to our lives. They inspire us with their enthusiasm, amuse us with their antics, console us when the world has treated us unfairly, and never run out of new ways to earn our

[189]

affection and respect. Reduced to the printed page, this tribute sounds hopelessly mawkish, but, to paraphrase Rhett Butler, I frankly don't give a damn. Retrievers have meant all of this and more to me during the decades we've spent together. I'm not just being sentimental; I'm being honest.

Bottom line: I'd have trouble getting out of bed in the morning to go duck hunting without one of the Labs at my side, and most serious hunters I know feel the same way. And no discussion of the waterfowling world would be complete without a tip of the hat to our canine companions. So here's to the dogs.

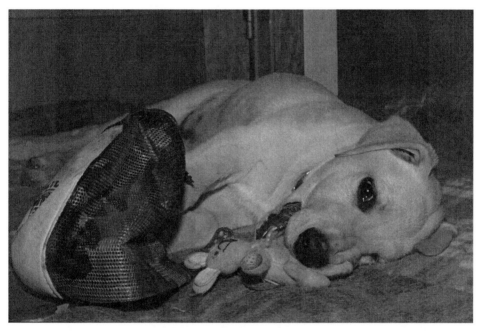

Rocky during his age of innocence.

Jake, doing the one thing he did well.

CHAPTER FORTY-THREE

Splash!

THE SNOW-LADEN PEAKS of the Alaska Range towering behind us to the west bespoke an endless winter, but down at sea level the early September morning felt positively balmy. Calm air and sunny skies hadn't produced much movement on the flats that morning, and I'd picked up and headed back to the cabin with nothing but a single widgeon in my game vest. All in all, it was shaping up as a fine day to do something other than hunt ducks.

Perhaps that's why the teal took me by such surprise. The tidal gut's overhanging bank stood high above the ebbing water and the birds exploded directly beneath me when I stepped up to scan the surface of the river. Caught off guard and burdened by a bag of decoys, I missed like an amateur with my first barrel. But I connected with my second, leaving a green-wing dead on the water and drifting away rapidly toward Cook Inlet.

As if Skykomish was about to let that happen… Under the circumstances, I wouldn't have been too upset had he chosen to run the bank, but that was never Sky's style. As soon as I issued the command to fetch, he launched like a cruise missile, apparently indifferent to the 10 vertical feet separating him from the falling tide. After an incredible hang time, he impacted the mixture of brine and ooze below in a glorious detonation of spray that reached all the way up the bank. The rest of the retrieve, and the morning, all proved an anti-climax, not that it needed to be anything more.

When I finally loaded the airplane and headed for home, I had to acknowledge that I'd spent the night in the wilderness just so I could watch a Labrador retriever jump off a bank into a glorified mud puddle. And I wouldn't have missed it for the world.

I've always found a determined retriever's water entry one of the most dramatic moments in outdoor sport. Theoretically, a dog's eagerness to attack the water might equate with fewer lost birds, but that's a secondary consideration. A spectacular water entry is both dramatic and unnecessary, and that lack of necessity lies at the heart of the matter. Fundamentally impossible to train, great entries arise from within. Dogs don't offer them because they have to, but because they want to, and they want to because of their love of the hunt.

Courage and enthusiasm form obvious components of a heart-stopping entry, but the dogs that do it best offer something subtler about the transition from land to water: disregard for any notion of transition at all. The best simply refuse to acknowledge a distinction between the two elements, as if they belong to both worlds equally. That attitude, in turn, helps define the essential character of the retrieving breeds.

Different dogs bring varying styles to this art form, and I find it interesting to note that the most efficient retrievers don't always demonstrate the most exciting water entries and vice versa. Sky had it all, but Sonny, another favorite, often looked lazy when he launched. Among my own dogs, none had an entry to match Jake, who was otherwise hard of head and mouth and unpleasant company in the blind. Credit his spectacular entries for saving him from the free-to-a-good-home column.

In our circle, the title of all-time best still goes to the late, great Lester, a Chessie owned and trained by a longtime hunting partner. Lester's catalog of redeeming virtues was even shorter than Jake's, but given a line off the Golden Gate bridge I have no doubt he would have taken it and hit the water swimming. Like any grand performer, Lester had to be seen in action to be believed. On slow mornings in the blind, we would sometimes grade entries as if the dogs were divers or gymnasts. While it may theoretically be impossible to achieve a perfect 10 Lester often came close, and for that I'll always remember him fondly.

Perhaps that's the element of the water entry that sets it apart from other canine accomplishments we witness in the field. So much has been written about training retrievers to mark and handle that even when they do so exceptionally their performances somehow seem a matter of course. True measures of exception can never be taught. "There are no tricks," a French wag once observed of another compelling activity. "There is only enthusiasm."

Indeed, nothing burns its way into the human memory like enthusiasm, ensuring our recollection of the dogs that have served us long after they are dead and gone.

Sonny enjoying his old age.

CHAPTER FORTY-FOUR

House Dogs

AFTER PUTTING Rocky through his paces with whistle and dummy on the lawn one summer day, I kenneled him and walked back inside the house only to discover that a disaster had taken place during my brief absence.

It didn't take long to analyze the crime scene. To avoid unnecessary distraction during the training session, I'd left Kenai, Rocky's son, unsupervised in my office. Although still a puppy in terms of calendar and temperament, Kenai was already pushing 90 lean pounds on the scale, which translates into a lot of kinetic energy when fueled by typical Labrador enthusiasm. At the sound of my whistle outside, Kenai had left his favorite resting spot beside my desk to critique the proceedings. The best vantage turned out to be from the top of Lori's desk in front of the third floor picture window.

Readers familiar with Labs will have little difficulty visualizing the results of his cheerleading. Lori's computer lay upended on the floor, emitting dying beeps. The contents of her In and Out boxes looked as if they had been shuffled by a tornado. Numerous items of sentimental value to my endlessly tolerant spouse bore telltale canine tooth marks, and dog slobber coated the picture window. Meanwhile, the perpetrator lay curled up serenely on the floor like a fallen canine angel.

While I've always taken a casual attitude toward conventional notions of household order, Lori appreciates organization and cleanliness enough for both of us. Since she was due back from errands in town at any moment, I felt like one of the kids in *The Cat in the Hat*, with the moment of adult reckoning bearing down relentlessly. I didn't have time to think about disciplining the dog. Unless I magically found a way to restore order from chaos quickly, the two of us would have all the time in the world to discuss the matter together in the kennel, where I sensed we'd both soon be banished for life.

The notion that **gun dogs** should even be allowed in the house, much less be given license **to reign** there, defies entrenched wisdom. In his classic text on retriever training, James Lamb Free sternly cautioned against the practice while advising novices to have their charges fed by servants, to dispel any idea that contact between dog and handler meant something other than work. Since the servants have been on strike around our place for many generations I always found this council of limited practical value, but it still speaks volumes about the way our predecessors viewed their relationships with working retrievers.

Not that this rigid approach lacks practical reasons to recommend it. Never mind theoretical concerns about casual exposure to human company compromising a dog's focus on training. Retrievers are big animals, and big animals at close quarters inevitably threaten domestic order no matter how amiable their personalities. Furthermore, there's an impish quality to most retrievers that renders their capacity for well-intended mischief greater than the sum of its parts. How else to explain those muddy paw prints in so many unlikely places, or a typical Lab puppy's capacity to locate and shred items as diverse as first edition books and rare fly-tying materials?

But I have to admit that I've always been a sucker for Labs hanging around underfoot. I just plain enjoy their company. They demonstrate a unique ability to express enthusiasm without becoming overbearing and impose fewer demands upon my tolerance than most people I know. Why waste companions like that by consigning them full time to the kennel?

My own Labs all made very different houseguests. Sonny, for example, always seemed content to retreat to a favorite *querencia* and keep unobtrusively to himself. Sky found devious means to create puppyish mischief all the way into his dotage. Rocky's manners are impeccable, but he follows me around like a yellow shadow, seldom straying out of ear-scratching distance even when I'm working long hours at my desk. But each found a way to remind me why retrievers are more than machines designed to improve the harvest every fall, and I can't help but think how much more boring household life would have been without them.

"How was your trip to town, honey?" I asked cheerfully when Lori walked back through the door.

"What's wrong?" she replied, confirming that my ability to feign innocence in the face of feminine authority figures hasn't improved much since my mother used to grill me about skipping school to go hunting when I was a kid.

"Nothing," I protested as I helped put away groceries with what may have been a little too much willingness to be useful. When she finally ascended the stairs, I held my breath and shot a conspiratorial glance at Kenai, secure in the knowledge that whatever happened next was going to happen to both of us.

And that may be the best argument of all in favor of treating our retrievers as friends.

Lori and Yaeger with a mixed bag of sea ducks.

CHAPTER FORTY-FIVE

Take It or Leave It

DESPITE DECADES OF EXPERIENCE WITH LABS, a surprising number of the most spectacular canine performances I've ever witnessed in the water came courtesy of a different breed: the Chesapeake Bay retriever. From frozen ponds in Montana to crashing surf along the Alaska coast, I've watched friends' Chessies face incredible challenges and make them look routine. All of which makes me wonder how two breeds with such similar origins and job descriptions could have taken such divergent paths in the popular imagination.

A century ago, retrieving breeds remained marginalized by the sporting dog establishment, and today the Chessie still enjoys few enthusiasts outside the ranks of dedicated waterfowlers. The Lab, however, has become the most popular dog in America according to AKC registration statistics. Hard to believe the two breeds occupied the same social niche so recently.

Among hunters, opinions of Chesapeake Bay retrievers are like certain parts of the human anatomy: everybody seems to have one. Those devoted to other breeds complain about everything from Chessies' manners to their smell, charges they're as likely to raise against Chessie owners as their dogs, at least once those owners have left the room. Those who own and handle Chessies usually defend their dogs with nearly religious conviction. Listening to members of the two camps discuss Chessies can make impartial participants in the discussion wonder if they're talking about the same breed.

Few reasonable observers will deny that Chessies can be stubborn. (Of course, some Chessie owners will, but they're seldom reasonable observers, and tend to be stubborn themselves.) I've often seen hunting partners' Chessies reduce them to despair just to win pointless battles of will that even my most hardheaded Labs would have abandoned far earlier. But those hunting partners still take to the field each fall with Chessies at their side, which should say something about the dynamics between Chessie enthusiasts and the breed.

My own experience doesn't support the more serious complaints commonly leveled against Chessies. I've never met a truly mean one, although I'm not ready to fight a Chessie over the contents of the food dish. They seem no more likely than Labs to scrap with other dogs, although they may be more likely to win. I've known many that were great with children. And while they're arguably the most specialized of the waterfowling breeds, I've hunted over several that were accomplished in upland cover as well.

However, I also believe that most Chessies view people in ways Labs can't imagine. While eagerness to please practically defines the Lab's personality, even the most likable Chessies demonstrate a certain emotional distance. Their relationships with their owners tend to take the form of mutually beneficial partnerships. They serve because they want something (usually an opportunity to retrieve). They greet with indifference expressions of displeasure that would at least temporarily break a Lab's heart. Every Chessie I've hunted with has eventually offered me a simple choice: take it or leave it. And they seldom waste hunting time brooding over hurt feelings, yours or theirs.

Appreciating any sporting breed requires seeing the dogs perform the task for which they were born and bred. In the Chessie's case, that means retrieving waterfowl in large, cold bodies of water. A century ago, plenty of American waterfowling took place on the sea, but nowadays even avid duck hunters can end their careers without feeling the pull of the tides. And that means never enjoying an opportunity to see Chessies do what they do best.

Chessies enjoy a nearly mystical relationship with the sea. Near the tide line, they act like pilgrims at the end of a long journey. They long to call the ocean home and once they're close, it becomes practically impossible to keep them out of it. They invent excuses to immerse themselves in salt water, and some of their notorious diffidence disappears once they leave shore. The sea is real Chessie habitat, and those who have never seen them perform there can't be truly qualified to comment on the breed.

Asked to pick one adjective to summarize the Lab's character, I'd consider several choices: eager, loyal, enthusiastic, devoted. Chessies make that hypothetical problem far easier. They're just plain tough. My old friend Bob May once took his young female Coco along on a commercial fishing trip. A day's run from home on the north side of Kodiak, he realized that she was no longer aboard. He searched the shore for days before giving her up for dead. A month later, she showed up on his porch after traveling nearly a hundred miles along one of the most rugged coastlines in the world.

Now, that's a Chessie. The breed may never duplicate the Lab's incursion into suburban America, but they have their character and their place. And as the dogs themselves might say: Take it or leave it.

Rocky and Lori enjoying the morning hatch on our local spring creek.

CHAPTER FORTY-SIX

Whose Best Friend?

WITH GRAY SCUD OBSCURING THE LANDSCAPE and horizontal rain driving against the windows of the tiny cabin, the October cold front made a persuasive argument for turning up the oil stove and crawling back inside my sleeping bag. But I wanted to go duck hunting and so did Sky, my aging yellow Labrador. After all, that was the mission we'd flown across Cook Inlet to accomplish. Using concern over the airplane's security in the wind as an excuse to venture outside, I climbed into my woolens and opened the door to the weather. Once I'd confirmed that the Cub had survived the night in its tie-downs, I rounded up my shotgun and a pack full of decoys, and then the dog and I set off together across the tide flats.

No place enforces the notion of solitude like wilderness Alaska, for reasons that go beyond the bear tracks and the weather. It's the delicious loneliness of the place that defines the mood, the realization that there's no one around to bother you – or to help you. Isolation in a wilderness camp with bad company can be an excruciating experience, but sharing one with others whose companionship you enjoy infuses the idea of friendship with new meaning. And it doesn't really matter whether good company walks on two legs or four.

In fact, I'm not sure I would have made it out of the sleeping bag that morning if it hadn't been for Sky. His incessant tail-wagging back in the cabin's dim interior reminded me how badly he wanted to hunt, and it's never easy to say no to that kind of enthusiasm. Sometimes the real value of hunting dogs lies in their ability to discourage the rest of us from taking the easy way out.

Because of the weather we didn't travel far that morning, but we didn't have to. A short hike across the flats brought us to the edge of a brackish slough where I tossed out a handful of decoys and huddled down in the dead grass next to the dog. The storm had brought waves of waterfowl down from the interior and little flocks of green-wings, pintails, and mallards dropped their landing gear and floated into our spread until I'd shot what I cared to shoot. I thought about braving the elements long enough to add a few geese to the bag, but the dampness seeping in around the edges of my rain gear convinced me it was time to declare victory and withdraw from the field. On the hike back to the security of the cabin, even Skykomish seemed comfortable with the decision.

By mutual agreement with my absent hunting partners, we weren't supposed to let dogs into the hunting cabin, and a row of airline dog boxes lined the porch to accommodate our canine friends. While I'd already fudged on this rule the night before, there's a big difference between a clean, dry dog and a wet one covered with tidal mud after a morning of vigorous hunting. But Sky had served me too well that day to be consigned to a cold kennel. Out on the porch, I toweled him down with an old shirt and bade him enter while I prepared a breakfast of braised teal and canned beans appropriated from the store of staples we kept under the kitchen table. And as the heat from the oil stove filled the cabin with the smell of wet wool and wet dog, we sat down to one of the best hot meals in memory… together.

A few years later, the American Kennel Club accepted over 100,000 registration applications for Labrador retrievers, making the Lab the country's most popular dog breed, as it has remained ever since. Strange as it may seem to those of us who find retrievers and waterfowling inseparable, most of those dogs will never hear a shotgun's bark or gaze eagerly overhead as sets of wings cut the air. I'm not sure just what to make of this development.

Most of those dogs will enjoy happy lives in good homes, and many will find service in a variety of capacities ranging from guide dog to law enforcement to backyard babysitter. But will they ever really enjoy the opportunity to be Labs, and will their owners be able to say they know their charges? I'm skeptical. I recently had a non-hunting Lab owner ask me how anyone could make dogs jump into icy water to fetch ducks. Had she truly known the breed, she might have asked how anyone could refuse to let them.

For years, our military, which trains the finest fighting forces in the world, has understood the essential relationship between *espirit de corps* and shared challenges. Sky and I understood that relationship well that morning, and I feel confident that I speak for both of us.

Rocky, off to an early start.

CHAPTER FORTY-SEVEN

A Brief History
of Labs

DESPITE THE CLOSE RELATIONSHIP I've always enjoyed with my parents, I'm embarrassed to admit how little I know of my own genealogy. Both my grandfathers were gone long before I was born, and I retain no memory of my paternal grandmother. I came from wayward pioneer stock on both sides, and no one ever bothered keeping family records. This deficit has left me with a keen appreciation for the value of knowing one's past.

How ironic that I know so much about the background of my dogs! Thanks to meticulous record keeping by the American Kennel Club, I can easily learn more about Rocky's great-great grandmother than I've ever known about my own. But go back more than a century in time, a mere three generations in human terms, and matters become more complicated.

Even as our most popular dog breed, the Labrador retriever enjoys a complex and occasionally murky history. Little wonder. While the breed's recent records remain well documented, its remote origins involved events on both sides of the Atlantic, often under obscure circumstances. But since you can't understand today's Labs without understanding their history, let's take a brief chronological look at the breed's origins and accomplishments.

Before we begin to review this timeline, let me remind readers that I'm no investigative historian, largely because I'd rather spend my time in duck marshes than libraries. While I've added some original observations of my own, the chronology that follows largely derives from Richard Wolters' classic text *The Labrador Retriever*, and I wish to acknowledge my indebtedness.

1497 – Henry Cabot "discovers" Newfoundland. In fact, Basque whalers have operated in these waters for years, and two of Cabot's own countrymen, Robert Thorne and Hughe Elliot, beat him there as well.

1576 – British sportsman George Turbervile publishes his Booke of Hunting. His description of the St. Hubert's hound suggests that this breed may have been the Lab's European ancestor.

1600's – Devonshire fishermen begin to settle the Newfoundland coast, importing working water dogs to retrieve lines, nets, and even wayward fish. These hardy animals eventually evolve into the St. John's dog, a smaller and quicker breed than the Newfoundland.

1780 – In an effort to promote a fledgling sheep industry, the Governor of Newfoundland imposes heavy restrictions on dog ownership. The original St. John's dog declines precipitously in number, and only occasional dogs transported back to England remain to maintain breeding stock.

1809 – The Second Earl of Malmesbury describes using his "Newfoundland" (actually a St. John's dog) to hunt woodcock. His kennel will help maintain Labrador bloodlines throughout the 19th century.

1814 – British Col. P. Hawker publishes *Instructions to Young Sportsmen*. The text establishes the distinction between the St. John's dog and the Newfoundland and emphasizes the superiority of the former as a hunting dog.

1823 – English sporting artist Edward Landseer paints *Cora – A Labrador Bitch*, providing the first documented usage of the breed's modern name.

1839 – The Duke of Buccleuch introduces the St. John's dog to Scotland and refers to the breed as the Labrador.

1840 – Delabere Blaine publishes the *Encyclopedia of Rural Sports*, in which he notes: "The St. John's breed is preferred by sportsmen on every account, being smaller, more easily managed, and sagacious in the extreme."

1881 – Judge Owen Denny successfully introduces ring-necked pheasants to Oregon. The pheasant's popularity as a game bird will eventually produce a demand for a versatile flushing retriever in America.

1903 – The British Kennel Club officially recognizes the Labrador retriever as a distinct breed.

1906 – Major Maurice Portal's Lab Flapper wins the English Kennel Club's All-Age Stakes.

1916 – Viscount Knutsford and Lorna Countess Howe establish the Labrador Club in England.

1917 – Charles Meyer registers the first Labrador retriever with the American Kennel Club.

1931 – The American Labrador Retriever Club holds its first field trial.

1937 – Ducks Unlimited is founded, becoming the country's prototype wildlife habitat advocacy organization and ensuring a bright future for American waterfowl… and retrievers.

1939 – Paul Bakewell becomes the first amateur handler to win the National Club championship, an accomplishment he repeats for five consecutive years.

1951 – John Olin establishes Nilo Kennels. His King Buck becomes the breed's first American super-star and the first dog to appear on a federal duck stamp.

1973 – After spending my childhood and adolescence hunting

behind my father's German shorthairs, I acquire the family's first Labrador retriever while working as a medical intern in Montreal. Bogey, alas, does not prove "sagacious in the extreme".

1981 – Richard Wolters publishes *The Labrador Retriever*, the definitive modern study of the breed.

1991 – The Labrador retriever begins an enduring run as the American Kennel Club's most frequently registered breed.

The rest, as they say, is history.

Young girls: Gen Thomas and Becca.

CHAPTER FORTY-EIGHT

Warm Puppies

ALTHOUGH WE HUMANS LACK the olfactory awareness of the dogs we hunt with, I always find that the best way to get acquainted with a retriever puppy is with my nose. New puppies, like new trucks, come with a unique aroma made all the more appealing by the knowledge that it won't last for long before yielding to use and abuse in the case of the truck and whatever is available to roll in on the part of the dog. Like the smell of wildflowers after a spring rain, you should enjoy such pleasant aromas while you can.

Kenai was the last Lab puppy to join the household, and I spent plenty of time sniffing him before I brought him home with us. Our Rocky had sired the litter, entitling us to the traditional pick of the lot. Over the years I've witnessed all kinds of rituals as prospective owners put puppies through their paces in search of signs of future greatness, most involving duck wings and studious observation of interactions among littermates. Long ago, I decided that it's all a crapshoot in the end, so in Kenai's case I simply picked the male that smelled the best. This method of selection may seem bizarre coming from someone with a scientific background, but pseudo-science is worse than no science at all. When in doubt, it never hurts to go with your heart… especially when puppies are involved.

Like most writers in my field, I hunt lean cover. Two thirds of the trade fiction titles sold in America every year are romance novels, a telling statistic that handily summarizes the general public's expectations in reading matter. Had I been able to bring myself to write bodice-rippers instead of hunting stories, I would probably be retired by now. But I've spent a lot more time shooting ducks than ripping bodices, and in accordance with the old dictum to write about what you know, I've stuck stubbornly to subjects grounded in the out of doors.

But occasionally I enjoy the opportunity to address a topic of more universal appeal, like puppies. And my own sentimentality toward the subject has nothing to do with either commercial writing potential or the expectation of future companionship in the duck blind. Sure, I envision the makings of an eager gun dog lurking inside every retriever puppy I see. But those projections have never stopped me from enjoying puppies just for being what they are: puppies.

Noted American philosopher Charles Schulz, whose work certainly reflects a better grasp of the zeitgeist than my own, once famously observed that happiness is a warm puppy. I think he was on to something. Granted, waterfowlers all envision challenging job descriptions for their puppies once the dogs mature, but a sense of where we're going down the line has only enhanced my own appreciation for the one cardinal characteristic all puppies share: innocence. That will vanish soon enough as well, so enjoy it, just like that new puppy smell, while you can.

Kenai is two years old now, his new puppy smell long gone right along with his innocence. Of course he's still capable of puppy behavior; the difference is that he now knows that he's not supposed to chew on my boots and that knowledge creates nothing but problems for both of us. But he's also learned about redemption, in his case through hard work in upland cover and daring plunges into icy water. Redemption,

I suppose, is what remains once you've lost your innocence. If only people could attain it as adeptly as retrievers.

Because of the differences in our biological clocks, we'll outlive most of our dogs. I've learned the hard way just how short the lifespan of a good retriever can be, and the great ones seem to go quicker than all the rest even if calendars and registration papers prove otherwise. The upside to this hard fact of life is that I always have a succession of Labs coming along in the kennel, and that means I rarely have to go more than a few years without enjoying a good, practical excuse to get down on the floor and enjoy that new puppy smell all over again.

Of course I'll envision some measure of greatness in each new arrival: another Sonny, perhaps, or another Sky. Those standards are unfair, and taken literally they will only guarantee disappointment. But I've also learned through experience to identify the likable side of every dog that comes along and to appreciate whatever he or she eventually has to offer.

And even on the bad days when nothing seems to be going right, I can always close my eyes and remember that new puppy smell and everything it promised. Evoke that image keenly enough and the bad days will seem few and far between.

Kenai in a rare reflective mood.

CHAPTER FORTY-NINE

The Five Dollar Bet

Had a dog and his name was Blue.
Bet you five dollars he's a good dog, too.

—Traditional Appalachian folk song

THIS PLAINTIVE CHALLENGE, best accompanied by a steel string guitar and a bottle of whiskey with or without a seal across the top, raises a fundamental question. What is a good dog, anyway?

Acknowledging 50 years of experience with gun dogs isn't easy for a man who still considers himself young, but that's the only perspective I bring to the table. Over those years I've raised and trained several dozen dogs I'd call good and a couple I'd call great, although not everyone would share those opinions. One of the good ones was even named Blue, but he was a hound and so beyond the scope of this discussion. What made the good ones good, and how did they differ from the rest?

In the retriever world, field trials and hunt tests have gone a long way toward eliminating subjectivity from the discussion. Both set reasonable, practical standards for waterfowl dogs, and it's hard to imagine a successful participant that wouldn't win that five-dollar bet.

But I've always considered evaluation of a dog's abilities by others' standards, no matter how fairly applied, a sufficient rather than a necessary qualification for entry into the good dog category.

Ability in the field, however defined, is obviously an important part of being a good dog, and a retriever that never masters the basics isn't going to make the grade no matter what its other assets. But some of the best dogs I've hunted with weren't necessarily the most stylish. Several of them (my yellow Lab, Skykomish, and Bob May's Chessie, Yaeger, come to mind) wouldn't have provided anyone much competition in a field trial. Instead, they solidified their reputations by completing several retrieves every season that seemed utterly impossible at the time, typically involving various combinations of wounded birds, big water, and exceptionally adverse conditions. Witness just one of those performances and you'd be ready to concede the bet and reach into your wallet.

Other good dogs, like Rocky, one of my current Labs, lack that instinct for the spectacular but compensate through steady, quietly talented performances throughout one long season after another. Just as any major league utility infielder can make tough grounders look routine, these dogs make it easy to take their workmanship for granted. The best way to appreciate what they've been doing for you all along is to spend a morning in a blind with a genuine bonehead or a naïve youngster. The next time you hunt with your old, reliable standby, you'll realize how much talent was operating under your nose all along.

Formal evaluations of a retriever's abilities lack the means to quantify the dog's worth as a companion in the field. No wonder; it's usually impossible to appreciate those attributes from any distance. But a retriever that will sit quietly at your side and scan the sky for hours on end even when the ducks aren't flying always has a leg up on the competition in my book, even if the dog won't handle crisply at 200 yards. Most of the time we spend hunting waterfowl doesn't involve shooting or retrieving. A good dog should always make that time pass more pleasantly.

This principle illustrates one of the essential limitations of letting others decide whether or not your dog is a good one. A judge can assess a retriever's water entry and marking ability, which are on display for all to see. But how does a stranger appreciate, much less quantify, a dog's ability to make a long morning in a quiet blind a memorable experience? That's a difficult task, even though most veteran waterfowlers concur, at least in private, that personality counts as much as performance in the distinction between good dogs and also-rans. And since the elements of canine personality that count, such as enthusiasm, courage, loyalty, and eagerness to please, devolve quickly into the warm and fuzzy, it's no wonder no one has figured out how to add them up at the end of the day.

What we don't express about our dogs often matters as much or more than what we do. Sentimentality is still an awkward character trait in hunting circles. Most of us find it easier to talk about a dog's nose than a dog's heart. Granted, this observation sounds suspiciously like the buildup to a sappy episode of talk show psycho-babble: *Wet Retrievers and the Hunters Who Love Them*, perhaps. But maybe we do need to get in touch with our inner feelings about our dogs and express them more openly. For when the final whistle blast has faded from the marsh and the last greenhead has been delivered to hand, those feelings will likely determine more about how the dog will fare in the memory than any technical element of its performance as a retriever.

Some may remember the final verses of the musical elegy that introduced this piece, in which the narrator digs Blue's grave with a golden spade and lowers him down with a silver chain before concluding:

Here Blue, you good dog you.
Here, Blue. I'm coming too.

That Blue hunted coons and possums, not geese and teal, but he still has something to teach us. The partnership between hunters and their dogs antedates every technological advance our species has made including the wheel. In the beginning this relationship was no doubt purely functional, symbiosis designed to put more meat in the bellies of man and dog alike. But the written record, from cave walls to Shakespeare, Fielding, Faulkner, and beyond, documents the development of progressively deeper bonds. While their nature may be difficult to articulate, their strength remains an integral part of the waterfowling world.

At the end of the last season, we'll all be coming too. Perhaps the good dogs are simply those that help make the journey more rewarding.

Rocky with a late season greenhead.

CHAPTER FIFTY

All in the Family

'TWAS THE NIGHT BEFORE CHRISTMAS... and the absence of stirring mice didn't bother me one bit. We sure could have used some birds though. For two solid hours, old Sonny and I had sat side be side on the log and shivered in silence. Despite "perfect" conditions (sleet, fog, and a non-existent dew point spread), the skies had remained empty over the little slough, and with moisture starting to seep through my outerwear I was almost ready to pick up the decoys and head home to stockings and eggnog. But three days past the winter solstice, the kids would scarcely be home from school by the end of legal shooting light, so I decided to stick it out until the bitter end.

Good decision. There was still plenty of light left to distinguish drakes from hens when the mallards finally started to pour in from the fields, and with a drought era three-greenhead limit in effect it took less time to kill the birds than to tell the tale. When the last drake hit the water, I leaned my empty shotgun against the fallen cottonwood and sat back to watch the dog work. After enduring right along beside me, Sonny had earned an audience as surely as I'd earned the mallards.

None of the retrieves demanded much technically, but Sonny was getting to be an old dog by then and I had the feeling that the third bird might be his last. Back home in the kennel young Rocky was showing every sign of developing into a worthy replacement, but you can never really replace a Labrador retriever. By the time Sonny dropped the final bird into my outstretched hand and treated me to a shower of flying spray, I knew that staying had been the right decision for both of us.

Lori had sent me out of the house with a short list of last minute needs for the family dinner brewing back home, and I knew better than to drive past the grocery store without stopping. Fortunately, folks around town are used to seeing me dressed in waders. "It's Christmas Eve, Doc!" the woman behind the cash register observed cheerfully as I fumbled with my wallet. "I thought you'd be home with your family!"

"What makes you think I wasn't?" I replied.

Hunting dogs represent mankind's first historical attempt to enter into a cooperative working relationship with other animals. Artists have celebrated the value of that partnership from the walls of pharaohs' tombs to the tapestries of medieval Europe. Writers too, from King Lear's canine imagery to Fielding's Squire Westin romping with his hounds. While there sometimes seems little left to add, I would make an argument for the unique nature of the relationships that develop between waterfowlers and their retrievers.

Lest readers assume hopeless bias on my part, I should point out that I grew up with pointers, have hunted upland game with every kind of bird dog imaginable, and still keep cougar hounds in the kennel right next to the Labs. I've enjoyed all of them and loved most of them, minus allowances for the usual canine misbehavior to which all breeds are susceptible. But none has aroused the same emotional response as my retrievers, and therein lies the basis for an attachment that goes beyond crisp handling and spectacular water entries.

And it's not just me. I can't count the number of duck hunters who have told me they wouldn't bother putting on their boots to shoot a limit of birds if they couldn't take their favorite retriever along. Of course we all know upland hunters devoted to their bird dogs, but the nature of the relationship seems different. Pointers are hunting companions. Retrievers are family.

Part of the credit goes to the dogs themselves. The Labrador retriever has officially been the country's most popular breed for years now, and most of those Lab owners hunt seldom if ever. I attribute the Lab's winning personality to selective breeding during the early days when retrievers developed as working dogs in the fishing industry off the coast of Newfoundland. After all, who would want to spend a week in a cramped dory with a pit bull?

But the nature of waterfowl hunting contributes to these relationships as well. In blinds and boats, duck hunting often requires dogs and hunters to share close quarters for long periods of time, often under uncomfortable conditions. As football coaches and drill sergeants have long known, nothing produces camaraderie and teamwork like hardship endured in close proximity. There's no place like a duck blind on a frigid morning to discover the identity of your real friends.

As often as not, mine turn out to be retrievers. No wonder they're part of the family.

Don and Rocky, both in their prime.

CHAPTER FIFTY-ONE

In His Prime

ONE WOULD THINK that after 30 years here I'd know the location of every puddle in the county capable of holding a duck. But as Lori and I drove back from a pheasant hunt one October afternoon, I spotted a dam I'd never noticed before a mile off the gravel road. Detouring toward the nearest high ground for a better look, I could scarcely contain my excitement. The 20-acre pond was black with ducks.

Since we had no idea who owned the property, days of detective work followed. One of Lori's hospital co-workers living nearby gave us the critical lead. I called the ranch family, and it turns out I'd done some medical work for them years ago. Everything must have turned out fine, for we quickly received permission to hunt the pond.

A wise hunter might have waited for a cold, blustery day, but the prospect of hunting new places can get the better of my judgment. Besides, I was eager to give Rocky some waterfowl work before northern birds began to arrive. Dark-thirty the following morning found us tossing blocks into the pond beneath clear skies that promised a gorgeous prairie sunrise: great weather for casual conversation, but hardly promising for limits of waterfowl. Lori and I knew better than to complain. On a hunch, I'd brought a dozen goose shells along, and once we had them placed along the water's edge we settled back into the grass to wait.

During my original reconnaissance, I thought I'd seen divers in the air over the pond. Because of the distance I couldn't identify them precisely, but any diver would be a rare bonus here in the land of puddle ducks. I looked forward to seeing what birds were using the pond almost as much as to shooting them. Ten minutes before legal shooting light, two flocks of what appeared to be redheads began to circle the pond, silhouetted against the dull glow of the impending sunrise. Shotgun unloaded, I felt perfectly content to watch the aerial display.

By the time shooting light arrived, the ducks had departed and I began to resign myself to a philosophical morning. Suddenly a single brr-ONK rose from the sky behind us. I knew from the tone of the call that the goose was practically overhead, but could only freeze and hope it turned into the wind toward the decoys. "Stay!" I whispered unnecessarily to the dog. When the lone honker began to settle toward the pond, I rose to one knee and shot it.

When the goose hit the water swimming, I knew that Rocky had some serious work ahead. By the time I gave him the command he'd been longing for all morning, the goose was digging for the reeds on the opposite shore like an Olympic swimmer. Halfway across the pond, Rocky lost sight of the bird and turned back to me for directions. I'd walked to the top of the dam so he could see me better, and when I shouted "Back!" and gave him an overhand signal, he resumed course. By this time we had lost track of the goose; the rest was up to Rocky. But we had the right dog for the job. When he reappeared on the far shoreline 10 minutes later, we could plainly see the goose in his mouth.

Twenty minutes later, he had an opportunity to repeat the performance. A flock of redheads had reappeared, and after they'd circled the pond several times without paying any attention to our decoys, I pass-shot one. Once again, Rocky made the long retrieve on the diving cripple look easy.

The next hour passed quietly, giving me lots of opportunity

to think about dogs. Rocky's puppy years still seemed like yesterday. Both his weaknesses and his strengths had solidified over the last two seasons, as he remained tentative in upland cover while developing a quiet sense of command in the duck blind. It was time to accept him for what he had become: a tag-along pheasant retriever and a stalwart on waterfowl. I'll accept that tradeoff any day.

Standard dog-year calculations made Rocky almost 20 years younger than I was, although, like all dogs, he was gaining fast. That was still early middle age for him, but it marked prime time for a retriever: old enough to know what to do but still young enough to do it. His glory years would pass quickly, but I meant to enjoy them right along with him.

After a pair of gadwalls floated into the decoys and provided easy work for all of us, we decided to pick up early. We could have stayed longer and shot more, but no one needed to. We'd come for the dog, and some performances don't require encores.

Yaeger, ready for action.

CHAPTER FIFTY-TWO

Cruel Seas

GREAT RETRIEVES are like great art: difficult to define, they're still obvious when you see them. While some reflect brilliance of training and technique, the most memorable appeal directly to the deeper elements of the human brain responsible for a spectrum of emotions ranging from admiration to terror. Good retrieves leave handlers asking: How did the dog do that? Great ones leave them speechless.

With plenty of miles on my waterfowling odometer, I've seen plenty of memorable canine performances, most courtesy of my own Labs. Outstanding dogs made some of those retrieves, while others represented triumphs by boneheads that briefly found a way to hunt beyond their true skill level. But bragging up your own dogs can quickly grow tedious, so I'm going to pay tribute to a friend's retriever rather than one of mine: Yaeger, a tough Chessie who lived in Whale Pass, Alaska with my old friend Bob May.

The waters around Whale Pass could serve as a laboratory for the study of applied Darwinian theory. When the North Pacific decides to serve our continent some nasty weather, the Kodiak archipelago is usually one the first places to take it on the chin. High winds and strong tides can turn calm seas into a maelstrom in minutes. This country is tough on all its inhabitants, none more so than working water dogs.

I can't remember exactly when this hunt took place, probably because the Kodiak shoreline looks pretty much the same all fall: gray, wet, and foreboding. Bob had some work to do around his place, but he insisted that Lori and I go hunting without him. Yaeger never cared much who he hunted with as long as he got to hunt, and he ranged happily along beside us as we hiked a mile through the forest from Bob's house to Whale Island's northwest shore. We meant to set up for mallards on a small tidal lagoon, but as soon as we reached the beach we could see long lines of sea ducks trading back and forth near the mouth of the pass and decided to pitch our decoys into the surf instead.

Over the next hour, several sets of goldeneyes and scoters veered into range, providing some nifty shooting for us and routine retrieves for Yaeger. The sea in front of the beach looked no more dangerous than usual, but I couldn't see around the corner into the pass.

When a pair of harlequins buzzed the edge of the decoys, I rose and killed the drake. Yaeger broke as usual; Bob always admitted that his performance owed more to instinct and heart than formal training. I noted immediately that dog and bird were converging a lot more slowly than they had on earlier retrieves. In fact, the tide had built to a crescendo, and with the wind freshening, the current was rapidly sweeping the fallen bird around the point into the pass.

Whistling proved futile. The dog couldn't hear me over the noise of the wind and sea and probably would have ignored me anyway. Feeling uneasy, I leaned my shotgun against a stump and set off down the beach.

Huge, irregular standing waves greeted me when I rounded the point. The current inside the pass looked as if it was trying to scrub the barnacles off the rocks. I couldn't see the dog anywhere and my uneasiness began to evolve into dismay. An experienced seaman in a 50-foot vessel would have had trouble surviving a ride through that water, let alone a dog. Dejected, I returned to Lori and told her that I planned to hike the beach as far as possible in search of Yaeger. Truth is, I needed some time to decide how I was going to explain matters to Bob.

The shoreline inside the pass consisted of gravel beaches broken by low, rocky cliffs. By the time I'd scrambled through a half mile of clamshells and seaweed, my clothes were soaked in salt spray and my hands stung from scrapes and cuts. I forged on not because I thought I was going to find Yaeger alive, but because I knew that I would eventually have to be able to say I'd done my best.

Suddenly, a flicker of movement caught my eye down the beach. The visibility had dropped so sharply that I couldn't be certain what I'd seen at first, and I braced myself against the possibility of an encounter with a bear. Finally, a canine shape emerged from the gloom. When I shouted his name, Yaeger veered in my direction, spit the harlequin out on the sand, and continued back toward Lori and the blind as if he'd just fetched a newspaper from a suburban porch.

No big deal, those cold yellow eyes seemed to say as he trotted by, and perhaps it wasn't to him. But it certainly was to me.

Jake retrieving a mallard.

Section V

The Waterfowling Culture

Jewelry.

The
Waterfowling
Culture

THE WATERFOWLING CULTURE? Is this a joke?

Hardly. My Random House dictionary defines culture thus: "The quality in a person or society that arises from a concern for what is regarded as excellent in arts, letters, manners, scholarly pursuits etc." Look deeply enough beneath the layers of mud and feathers and you'll find concern for just those subjects on display when most duck hunters gather. In fact, compared to enthusiasts of two other outdoor pursuits that arouse my passion--fly-fishing and bowhunting big game--waterfowlers seem downright preoccupied by those qualities, admittedly an unlikely observation to make about folks who dress in waders and rise in the dark to bleat on duck calls.

The concise definition cited above omits one crucial element: history. Culture does not arrive overnight courtesy of UPS. Rather, it must steep over time and celebrate its own traditions, in which regard waterfowling occupies a unique position in the annals of outdoor sport. Duck hunters were establishing their history at a time when big game hunting was still about little more than putting meat on the table and a century before A River Runs Through It propelled fly-fishing from obscurity to the heart of modern fashion. That this long sense of tradition has resulted in enthusiasm more than snobbery remains a tribute to factors I have not yet been able to identify.

[235]

But history alone cannot explain waterfowlers' devotion to the esthetic, as opposed to merely practical, aspects of duck hunting. No other segment of the outdoor community produces artwork to rival a spirited duck stamp competition or a collection of vintage hand-carved decoys. No one else seems to understand the natural history of wildlife so well. Perhaps they're all just too busy.

In fact, the culture of waterfowling may derive as much from its leisurely pace as from its history. In contrast to many other sporting activities, duck hunting usually offers participants ample time to talk, observe, and reflect, even when they're hunting as hard as they can. It's difficult to feel "concern for what is regarded as excellent" when you're chasing bonefish across a flat or elk up a hill. The duck blind, on the other hand, can evoke the ambience of a salon or lecture hall, even though it's usually colder and wetter. And even when the birds arrive, the interruption seldom lasts for long.

Granted, most of these theories represent speculation. But waterfowling really is different, as I hope to prove with the brief look at art, cuisine, natural history and, above all, human relationships that follows. And if I fail to convince readers that a waterfowling culture really does exist, I'll eat a merganser.

As long as it's cooked right.

Diver decoys on Kodiak.

Getting ready for incoming Gulf Coast teal.

CHAPTER FIFTY-THREE

Cancelled Stamps

A RESERVED, THOUGHTFUL OUTDOORSMAN, Jim Borgreen has taught art to high school students in my Montana hometown for 30 years. And he practices what he teaches. Eight times, he finished runner-up in the annual contest that determined the painting featured on Montana's waterfowl stamp, an always-a-bridesmaid scenario that might have left a less philosophical artist discouraged. Fortunately, Borgreen persevered and eventually won three times, sending thousands of sportsmen into the field with his work in their wallets: paintings of canvasbacks in 1986, sandhills in 2002, and mallards in 2003.

Not that he earned anything tangible for his efforts. Cash payment to the winning artist? Zero. Until the last two years of the competition, the state also retained all rights to reproduce his winning images. He used to get a sheet of stamps for his trouble, but even that small perk eventually disappeared, leaving him to shell out $8.00 along with everyone else for a miniaturized version of his own painting so he could hunt ducks. Jim Borgreen spent all those long nights in his studio for one reason only: He loves waterfowl and the challenge of capturing their magic visually.

But not any more. After introducing an automated licensing

system, the state decided that the production and distribution of an actual duck stamp would be too costly to justify. Technically, Montana waterfowlers still get a "duck stamp", but it's nothing but a few extra letters generated when a computer spits out licenses. The cans, cranes and greenheads artists like Jim Borgreen once immortalized will fly no longer.

Somewhere in Helena, anonymous bean-counters evidently assumed no one would notice or care. Wrong...

Back when I was a kid still too young to hunt (a segment of my childhood that fortunately didn't last long) my father's purchase of his federal duck stamp every year became an important occasion. He would place each crisp, new stamp on his desk under a light for us to examine. We'd discuss the species of the year, and he'd tell a story or two about his experiences with it. Then he would sign it carefully on an obscure margin in order to preserve the image. These exercises taught me plenty of respect for three of the most important things in life: ducks, art, and fathers.

Duck stamps represent a distinctly American contribution to waterfowling traditions. I'm sure better ideas have come out of Washington over the years, but I'm hard pressed to think of a recent example. Any government program that supports both art and wildlife is automatically off to a great start. No wonder others eventually followed our federal government's lead. Thanks to overzealous bidding at a long string of Ducks Unlimited banquets, first-of-nation stamps and prints from all over the world now occupy the walls of our house. And many states eventually came on board with duck stamp programs of their own, as Montana did in 1979.

Raising revenues for wildlife has always been a worthy goal, but duck stamps accomplish much more. Despite the paucity of reward at the state level, these programs motivated thousands of artists to put forth their best, and I'm still idealistic enough to believe that all art benefits society for the same reason Mallory tackled Everest: because it's there. In a world awash in official documents, the notion that one can actually be visually compelling sounds downright visionary. Imagine what a kinder, gentler world we would inhabit if the design of our driver's licenses and income tax forms arose through spirited artistic competition.

In a more utilitarian vein, duck stamps represent a form of free advertising. Wildlife needs constituents, and it never hurts to promote its inherent beauty. Fifty years after the fact, I still remember the trips to the bird book and the stories my father told *a propos* of each year's new duck stamp. In an age when kids think truth comes from video games, we need those moments more than ever.

Granted, the world of sporting art will not likely collapse due to the demise of Montana's duck stamp program, but this decision represents part of a disturbing trend. A number of other states have recently announced plans to do away with duck stamps in favor of computer-generated equivalents, a bargain made in hell if ever their was one. The impetus is clear: Economic circumstances have drained many state coffers. But the solution to the problem is clear as well: Bump the cost of state stamps up a buck or two to cover the costs. Then remind the inevitable complainers that a few dollars in license fees still allow everyday Americans sporting opportunities reserved for nobility in most countries.

That seems a small price to pay in order to keep artists like Jim Borgreen busy trying to capture the spirit of the wild.

Daughter Gen, helping with the decoys.

CHAPTER FIFTY-FOUR

Traditions of Our Own

THE PINK EASTERN SKY dissolves slowly as sunrise floods the vast expanse of dry reeds with a golden glow. The air above the marsh lies crisp and still. Beside me on the wooden bench, Sonny offers the smell of wet fur and an eager whine of anticipation. Finally, the first flight of the morning appears as abstract dots silhouetted above the distant horizon, direction of flight indeterminate. But then each dot begins to enlarge slowly; the birds are inbound in response to the lure of the decoys and the greeting of the call. Even before the first shot, I can fix my position firmly in my mental atlas of time and space. There's no place like this in the world.

And I mean that literally. Our Third Rock from the Sun has been aptly described as the Water Planet, and ducks and geese know how to thrive virtually everywhere we've left them water to occupy. Many of our own most popular waterfowl species, including mallards, pintail, and teal, enjoy a remarkably worldwide distribution. But there's no place to appreciate them quite like home.

In the course of my travels, I've found ways to hunt ducks in Latin America, Africa, Siberia, and the south Pacific, and I've enjoyed the unique flavor of all those exotic waterfowling experiences. But in contrast to my overseas adventures with longbow and fly rod, hunting ducks in faraway places usually leaves me feeling vaguely homesick. Waterfowl and their pursuit have always provided a special means of defining the places I've chosen to live. And with all due respect, no one does ducks and duck hunting with quite the sense of tradition and ceremony we enjoy right here.

A number of important sporting traditions arose in North America. Which best defines our collective character? Possibilities abound. Baseball? Although I spent my early childhood next to the Hall of Fame in Cooperstown, I devoted more time to the study of black ducks than curve balls. A great game, but it takes a lot of people to play, and sitting around in a dugout waiting for something to happen isn't nearly as enjoyable as sitting around in a duck blind. Football? Not if you value your knees. Basketball? The options are inherently limited for short people who can't jump. So why not duck hunting?

History supports the concept. North Americans have been hunting ducks about as long as they've been doing anything, with the possible exception of arguing politics. The world's great retrieving breeds originated on our shores, as did the finest expression of the decoy carver's art. No one in the world prepares wild duck for the table with our own enthusiasm and imagination. We've always understood the importance of keeping waterfowl and their enjoyment accessible to ordinary citizens, and we led the way in the conservation of waterfowl resources for future generations, through the efforts of public and private sectors alike. For over two centuries, we've taken our ducks and geese seriously, and it shows.

Even in other countries that are home to strong populations of waterfowl, their pursuit often lacks the sense of tradition and gravity it enjoys in the United States and Canada. Africans regard ducks as an occasional diversion between big game hunts. In Siberia, ducks are just another potential source of soup. But on our own continent, waterfowling has evolved into a virtual way of life complete with all the trappings of cultural ceremony. From scouting new hunting areas to training dogs to working on local habitat restoration projects, the

[244]

faithful never seem to run out of ways to express their enthusiasm.

Back in the blind, the approaching dots have begun to acquire definition: profiles, colors, and wing beat patterns that define the birds as a mixed early season flock of gadwall and widgeon. The final chuckle from the call serves no benefit other than my own, as the birds obviously have the decoy spread locked into their guidance system. Fascinating despite its relative technical simplicity, the shooting itself passes like a dream, and Sonny finally gets to translate some of his unfocused canine enthusiasm into action. Think of experiences like this as bird watching enhanced by a special element of pageantry, a means of grounding its participants in generations' worth of what has come before.

And remember that there really is no place like home, especially for the duck hunter.

Homecoming: the senior members of the Thomas family at the Barker Ranch.

CHAPTER FIFTY-FIVE

Homecoming

IN CONTRAST TO THE WET, WEST SIDE of the Cascades where they live, the corner of the Columbia Basin where my parents do their waterfowling now measures its annual inches of rainfall in single digits, most of which seemed determined to fall on us that morning.

Lori and I had driven from Montana to join my folks on the Barker Ranch, a model Ducks Unlimited restoration project in which my folks have held an interest for years as noted earlier. I sensed that we were late as we started for the blind, and the sight of mallards circling the pond in legal shooting light aroused a momentary feeling of peevishness on my part. But Lori reminded me that the day belonged to my parents. Besides, my father assured us that the real action wouldn't start until the birds returned from the fields mid-morning, and it's hard to argue with anyone who has won a Nobel Prize.

Turns out he was right, as usual (as Lori pointed out, also as usual). After setting out the decoys and settling into the blind, we spent an hour talking hunting and family matters before a flight of pintails appeared overhead and made us forget everything but ducks.

In typical pintail fashion, they circled repeatedly without ever committing to land. Strictly on the honor system, my father and his hunting partners impose a fine for killing a pintail hen, although the threat of embarrassment worried me more than the money. Even in the low light, the drakes were easy to identify by silhouette, but I elected to remain conservative. The first flock eventually departed with no shots fired, only to be replaced by another.

With pintail numbers down back home, I certainly appreciated the rationale for voluntary restraint. I finally decided to forget about shooting and settle back to watch the show as more sprig appeared wheeling and teasing overhead. Suddenly, a blocky shape appeared at the tail end of yet another flight. "Drake mallard!" I hissed to my folks. "Take him!"

"Looks like a hen," Dad whispered back.

There was only one way to settle the discussion. Confident of my call, I abandoned filial courtesy, rose, and dropped the bird. Moments later, Rocky delivered the greenhead. It's nice to be right sometimes.

For the rest of the morning, we watched educated birds circle the spread, passing on numerous mallard hens while picking off enough greenheads, widgeon, and teal for a duck dinner or two. The pace of the shooting proved casual rather than furious, but the constant presence of ducks overhead seemed to suspend the passage of time. While we finished the morning short of limits, we scarcely had to remind ourselves that there is never a limit on good company and the pageantry of waterfowl.

Lori, Rocky, and I finished the day sharing a blind with Michael Crowder, the young biologist who manages wildlife on the property. He promised us a real show right after sundown and the possibility of fast shooting during the last half hour of legal light. When a greenhead gave the decoy spread one look too many just after our arrival, I rose and fired only to watch the bird shudder and sail into the corn a hundred yards away.

Young Rocky had enjoyed straightforward retrieving all day, and he seemed to welcome the opportunity for a real test. After taking a line to the area of the fall, he turned promptly in response to a whistle blast and charged off in the direction of my cast like an old veteran. When he finally emerged from the cover with the bird in his mouth, I felt a flush of satisfaction as I realized how far he'd come over the course of his second season.

We'd taken several more mallards by the time my wristwatch turned us into observers. At the end of legal light, we unloaded and settled back to enjoy the spectacular display overhead. As if on cue, waves of birds appeared from the darkening sky and circled the field in steadily lowering spirals. While I love to shoot and eat ducks as much as anyone, I've noticed over the years that I sometimes enjoy waterfowl even more when my gun is unloaded. Although we couldn't shoot, I knew I'd sleep better that night just knowing how many birds were there.

Thomas Wolfe observed that you can't go home again, and perhaps he was right. Time has altered the character of the places where I learned to hunt, and I could read a measure of that change in the lines on my father's face that fall. But on this homecoming visit, I found wildlife, our most fragile resource, not only enduring but thriving. An old axiom of wildlife biology holds that game only needs four things to prosper: clean air, clean water, ample food, and a place to live.

To which I would add a fifth: the determination of people who care.

Lori in a Gulf Coast blind.

CHAPTER FIFTY-SIX

Windows on the World

THE TEAL WERE LATE, and I was sweltering even though I'd stripped down to shirtsleeves. While bowhunting the hills nearby, I'd glassed several flocks of blue-wings using the little reservoir and decided to trade my morning elk hunt for an opportunity to secure a teal dinner before the birds departed south. Then as time wore on beneath silent skies, I began to question the wisdom of that decision, although the dog, shamefully neglected during the first weeks of bow season, couldn't have been happier.

As the air continued to warm, the waterline a dozen steps in front of my makeshift blind began to stir. Aquatic insects appeared, and a flock of meadowlarks swooped in to preen and bathe while I remained undetected in my bower of tumbleweed and sage. Finally, I recognized something truly different at the edge of the water: a mud puppy half again as long as my index finger.

But I wasn't the only one to notice the amphibian. Because I live in rattler country, the sight of a snake always makes me flinch even though this one was obviously benign, at least to me. But not to the salamander… After an admirable stalk, the little garter snake struck and then began to haul its oversized prize up the bank in my direction.

The sight of the size-6 snake trying to choke down the size-10 mud puppy proved so engrossing that I almost missed the overdue arrival of the teal. In response to old Sky's eager whine, I grabbed for my shotgun and barely managed to snap off a single shot before the flock rocketed back up into the blue. What should have been an easy double wound up as a long chase across the sage for Skykomish, not that the squandered opportunity left either of us particularly upset. The dog felt happy just to have one duck in his mouth again, and while I knew there would always be more teal, I suspected that I had just witnessed my first and last lethal encounter between a snake and a salamander.

Much as I loved hunting upland game when I was a kid, waterfowl cast a special spell right from the start, largely because of the nature of the places where we sought them. After a mile or two, hunting empty pheasant cover can start to feel like just another hike, but I always seemed to find something of interest to study from the duck blind. This naturalist's bounty derives in part from the nature of waterfowl habitat, since countless species as diverse as mallards and mud puppies have adapted specifically to profit from the resources wetlands provide. But another important factor operates as well, for duck blinds are the one venue that encourages wing-shooters to shut up and hold still. And as recognized by bowhunters and naturalists alike, the less you move, the more you see.

Not all parties share this sense of enchantment, beginning with the dogs. Retrievers crave action. Mine head to the blind with one thing in mind, and it isn't the study of natural history. Fortunately dogs don't get to vote, and those who have learned their manners provide little distraction no matter what they're thinking. But some of my human hunting partners are as focused on the hunting as the dogs, which is why I balance my blind time each fall between companionship and solitude. My friends have every right to tell the same hunting story for the 20th time, especially if it's a good one. But I reserve the right to opt for silence and introspection occasionally, for those are the times when I learn the most about the natural world as viewed from a true ringside seat.

Back when I lived in Alaska, a morning in a tide line blind often provided more action for my binoculars and bird book than my shotgun. From alcids to rare Asiatic strays, the complexity of the marine bird life on the Alaska coast never ceases to amaze, and on days when the shooting was slow I'd remind myself that serious birders travel to similar locations just to watch. Back on the high plains most of the ornithology is old hat, but that's never kept me from enjoying the sight of old birds doing new tricks, or making mental notes on the behavior of the myriad unrelated avian species that call good waterfall habitat home.

Don't let all this warmth and fuzziness fool anybody... I still love the tension of circling birds, the whump of the shotgun, and the drama of an enthusiastic water entry. But I've always held that the best hunters are good naturalists (and vice versa), as exemplified in the work of Aldo Leopold. Pressured to seek shortcuts on the path to "success", too many younger hunters have lost track of this principle.

I know no better place to rediscover it than the duck blind.

Mallard versus Nobel Laureate.

CHAPTER FIFTY-SEVEN

The Mentor's Art

THESE ARE THE THINGS I REMEMBER BEST about my first duck hunt: the eerie quality of the pre-dawn light, the slosh of the lake water against my father's waders as he packed me out to the blind slung over his shoulder like a sack of potatoes, my fear that I might fall down into the inky blackness below offset by the certainty that he'd never drop me, the eager whine of the dog, the tantalizing whistle of wings overhead, the hushed atmosphere inside the blind once we reached it, the sense of initiation into the secret society of duck hunters, and the gratitude I felt for having been allowed to join. And all this before shooting light even arrived…

These are the memories of a five year-old, which explains why I can't recall what kind of ducks wound up on the game strap or how well the dog handled, details central to the recollection of hunts recalled from an adult perspective. But even though these events took place nearly 60 years ago and I can't remember much of anything about the shooting, that trip out to the blind through the darkness—an epic adventure to me, a 30-yard walk through knee-deep water in reality—marked the beginning of two seminal themes that have altered my life ever since: duck hunting and coming of age outdoors in the company of my father.

Hunter numbers are declining nowadays. Amidst the hand-wringing, numerous theories have emerged to explain the phenomenon: the urbanization of American society, the rise of single parent households, the influence of celebrity animal rights advocates, distraction by the instant gratification video games afford the young. There's some truth to all of these concerns. But one factor central to our failure to recruit more young hunters into the ranks doesn't get the attention it deserves: a decline in the number of effective mentors.

The word mentor derives from the Greek. As students of Homer will recall, Mentor was the loyal adviser to whom Odysseus entrusted the education of his son Telemachus during his absence while he fought in the Trojan War. In modern usage, which began in 1699 with Francois Fenelon's *Les Adventures de Telemaque*, teaching ability forms a necessary but not a sufficient definition of the term. On my route from kindergarten through medical school and beyond, I encountered many good teachers but only a few mentors. They were the ones who not only taught but inspired, who recognized me not as a face in a classroom but a project worthy of individual attention despite my shortcomings. That's the kind of role model young hunters need today.

The creation of a new hunter involves elements of both nature and nurture, to phrase the issue in classic psychological terms. I am convinced that a gene—or more likely a complex series of genes—encoded in our makeup turns some of us into hunters no matter what. I base this conclusion on the observation that some of my staunchest hunting partners grew up in urban households in which no one cared in the least about hunting. Somehow, they made it happen despite the odds. We could use more of them today.

But all seeds grow best in the right environment, and all but the most exceptional potential hunters require some sort of mentoring. The mentor may be a parent, a relative, a family friend, or a casual acquaintance from the local sporting goods store, rod and gun club, or DU chapter. The mentoring may be casual or intense. All I know is that I was lucky enough to enjoy the best.

[256]

My father grew up dirt poor in rural Texas during the Great Depression, the only son of one of the last horse and buggy era rural physicians. No one in his family hunted, at least not seriously, but he took to the outdoors anyway. While my playmates were listening to nursery rhymes before they went to bed at night, I was seated on the couch in front of the fire listening to my father recount, in the great Southern tradition, stories from his childhood about catfish and possums and hound dogs, to my young mind indistinguishable in scope from the adventures described in the book he read aloud from most frequently, Col. James Corbett's *Man Eaters of India*. A good mentor can cast that kind of spell, and doesn't have to tell any lies to do it. Or at least not many.

By the time I made that fateful trip out to the duck blind I already knew something about catching brook trout and shooting a .22, but the pageantry—I can still think of no better word for it—I experienced that morning cast its own kind of spell over me throughout a childhood (which has never really ended) full of ruffed grouse, fly rods, bird dogs, horses, and trap lines. I always found duck hunting special for reasons that are still difficult to define. My father was something of a grouse and woodcock specialist, but he'd pass up an afternoon in the county's best upland cover just to sit beside me near a beaver pond while I hoped a teal flew in before dark. To my father's credit he always indulged me—another mark of the true mentor.

And what a time we had… My family lived in upstate New York then, and the waterfowling could hardly be called spectacular compared to what I've enjoyed later in the Pacific Northwest, Alaska, and Montana. Not that it mattered… I can still remember sitting on the floor of our canoe while my father paddled and smoked his pipe in the stern and my mother sat in the bow with her shotgun cradled across her lap, eager to see what lay waiting around the next bend in the creek. When we came home with a couple of woodies or teal it was a good day, and when we added a black duck or a mallard it was a great one. Those adventures taught me that you don't have to do a lot of shooting to enjoy yourself in the field, a principle that has served me well ever since.

Meanwhile, my father had embarked upon a labor of love for which I will never be able to repay him: teaching me how to shoot a shotgun. In the field, he was the best wing-shot I've ever seen, an impression that has never changed. While many good shots are not good teachers, he was an exception. I received a solid grounding in the fundamentals at an early age and was shooting with the top of the pack at our local skeet range by the time I was nine or ten, all because of his uncanny ability to analyze my mistakes and show me how to correct them. Nowadays when someone congratulates me for making a tough shot in the field, I just reply, "I learned from the best."

But doing things well in the outdoors isn't always the same as doing them right, and like the best of mentors he was enforcing that lesson at the same time he was teaching me how to get my feet in the right place before I shot. The highest compliment he could bestow on anyone in the outdoors was to declare them "a real woodsman", an honorific that implied skill and ethics in equal measure. I still remember the morning a teal dropped into the decoys by surprise and a casual acquaintance who had joined us for the day shot it on the water. My father didn't say a word, but he didn't have to. The temperature seemed to drop ten degrees instantaneously inside the blind. "Remember," he said to me once we'd reached home. "Real woodsmen don't shoot ducks on the water." The impression that statement made could not have been more forceful had he carried it down off a mountain engraved on stone tablets.

Idyllic as my Tom Sawyer childhood was in many ways, there still were rules. Like the best legislation, they were unambiguous and backed up by the promise of swift and certain enforcement. All my parents asked of me was that I complete my chores, bring home top grades, and stay out of trouble; then I got to go hunting. The third of these obligations proved by far the most difficult, especially as I approached adolescence. But there was no plea-bargaining in our household, and the sight of my father loading the truck to leave for the opening day of duck season without me provided powerful motivation to reform. Today's parents who feel frustrated by inability to control their kids' access to the Internet should take note.

By this time my family had moved to the Seattle area, where my father had taken a position as Chair of the University of Washington Medical School's Department of Oncology. The Columbia Basin became our primary waterfowl destination. We hunted public land, and the birds were smart. Sometimes we shot limits, and sometimes we didn't shoot anything. Patience, the virtue I'd learned from my father beside those beaver ponds in New York, served us well. The time we spent together was more important than the shooting anyway. I was a particularly rebellious teenager, but we always managed to declare a truce in our battle of wills long enough to go duck hunting.

When I finally completed high school, college, medical school, and internship, I wound up spending two years on a remote Montana Indian reservation. This position gave me my first opportunity to enjoy truly spectacular waterfowl hunting, and I was delighted to share it with my father, who by this time looked a whole lot wiser than he had when I was 16. Oddly enough, visits from my parents always seemed to take place during hunting season. A curious change occurred in our relationship in the field around that time. I sometimes knew more about the hunting than he did, and he no longer automatically made the decisions for both of us. He impressed me by accepting this development with pride rather than resentment. When a mentor has done the job right, the mentoring should become a two-way street.

Since I can't summarize all of my father's professional accomplishments here, I'll cut to the high point. In a story worthy of Horatio Alger, he completed his ascent from a hardscrabble upbringing by receiving the 1990 Nobel Prize in Medicine for his pioneering work in bone marrow transplantation, a once unimaginable technique that has now saved countless thousands of lives all around the world. This accomplishment required a remarkable amount of work and more sleepless nights than most of us can imagine, but I know something about that aspect of his story that his many admiring professional colleagues don't: No matter how hard he was working, he always had time to take his kids hunting.

Around this time he became involved in a project that has since provided him with a special sense of satisfaction: an ownership position in the Barker Ranch, a Columbia Basin property that, with help from Ducks Unlimited, has grown into a model of productive waterfowl habitat. Despite its distance from my Montana home, my wife Lori and I met my parents there regularly if briefly for years, and every trip to a blind still managed to evoke memories of that first fearsome voyage through the dark all those many seasons ago. But my father has always regarded the Barker Ranch as more than just a place to hunt ducks. He considers his involvement there a means of giving back to the waterfowl that have meant so much to us over the course of our lives. And perhaps it will be the place where another skillful mentor convinces some youngster that there is more to life than Facebook.

This has been a personal story, but it touches on themes that concern all of us. Wildlife cannot thrive without advocates, and advocates do not arise by spontaneous generation. Someone must be there to mentor, and I can only present my father as an example of how to do it right.

As of this writing, my father, now 91 years old, lives independently in the Seattle area with my mother, his partner in one of the strongest marriages imaginable, and Folly, the yellow Lab that my siblings and I bought him as a puppy following the last of his old bird dogs' death several years ago. Peripheral vascular disease cost him a leg last year, and the impact of that event has kept him out of the field ever since. My goal is to get him back to a duck blind on the Barker Ranch again, and words cannot convey how badly I'd like to make that happen. If I can, we won't even have to shoot any birds.

I'll be happy just to sit beside him on the bench, watch Folly fetch some sticks, and listen to a few more words of wisdom from the finest mentor I'll ever know.

CHAPTER FIFTY-EIGHT

Jewelry

AFTER A SLOW HOUR BENEATH EMPTY SKIES, my hunting partner and I had lapsed into an earnest discussion of politics or some equally pointless topic when Rocky's ears perked up and his gaze shot skyward. Absent that subtle warning, we might have been taken by surprise. In the event, we just had time to shift our feet into shooting position before the birds broke over the treetops and spiraled down toward the blocks.

Over the years I've developed a lengthy catalog of excuses for poor shooting, any number of which I could have evoked at the time: surprise, deference to my inexperienced companion, desire to avoid inadvertently shooting a hen mallard. But the fact is that I just plain missed with my first barrel, and even though I connected with my second I remained feeling vaguely peevish and incompetent.

As the rest of the little flock clawed its way back to altitude, two drakes lay in the decoys where there should have been four. Rocky made short work of the first retrieve, but as he stepped from the water with the second bird in his mouth, a dull glint of sunlight on metal caught my eye. One of us had killed a banded bird, and my momentary displeasure with my shooting vanished instantly.

My friend had never seen a duck band before, so I called time out to explain its significance. I was still holding forth when I saw Rocky's attention focused upward again and looked up to see another flock flaring overhead. No matter… the morning promised plenty of birds, and the discovery of a banded specimen in the bag always takes precedence over everyday events.

I still remember my first encounter with a bird wearing a duck band. I was sitting in a blind beside a pond in upstate New York when my father ceremoniously handed me a black duck the dog had just retrieved and instructed me to examine it closely. My delighted discovery of the band around its leg initiated much the same discourse I directed at my hunting partner beside that remote Montana slough five decades later, albeit fueled by more childish questions on my part. What was it? Where did it come from? How did it get there? All answered thoughtfully, of course, in a manner designed to make the world of waterfowl seem even more intriguing than ever.

My father even let me handle the paperwork when the time came. I'm sure the Fish and Wildlife Service would have been happy just to know where and when the bird fell. But (shades of things to come) I wrote a full-page description of the event, right down to the shot, the retrieve, and the color of the sunrise. And I must have caught some biologist on the right day, because the return envelope included a handwritten note encouraging my further interest in waterfowl in addition to the usual data regarding the time and place of the banding. If only that biologist knew.

Never a compulsive collector of objects (as opposed to experiences), I've unfortunately let almost all the duck bands I've retrieved over the years vanish into the coat pockets and dusty drawers that seem to consume more valuable little objects than they were ever designed to hold. Sometimes I regret that carelessness, especially when I'm hunting with a veteran waterfowler with dozens of bands strung on a call lanyard like beads on a necklace. Those folks always seem to have a story to go with every band, and they're usually the kind of stories that can get anyone through a slow morning in a blind.

I do have one band saved more or less in perpetuity, though. On the hunt for paradise ducks in New Zealand described in an earlier chapter, the first bird that fell to my borrowed shotgun wore a band. In contrast to most species in the animal kingdom, female paradise ducks look gaudier than their mates, and I took that strikingly marked hen back home to the taxidermist band and all. Unfortunately, I've never found a practical way to carry her into the blind with me on social hunting occasions, but on quiet days I often manage to work her and the band into the conversation anyway.

Taken at face value, there isn't much to a duck band: a strip of cheap metal, a series of stamped digits, an understated plea to make some anonymous biologist's distant efforts receive their just reward. But duck bands, like certain other small metal rings, mean so much more. They connect places and people with common passions and, especially here in North America, remind us how arbitrary borders are to wildlife. (Every banded bird I've killed in Montana came from Canada.)

The jewelry some ducks wear on their legs may not contain diamonds or pearls, but despite their simplicity duck bands should always serve to remind us how vast and complex the world of waterfowl really is.

Texas teal on a foggy Gulf Coast morning.

CHAPTER FIFTY-NINE

The Fog of War

WE ARRIVED AT THE BLIND that December morning to find the skies above Washington's Columbia Basin shrouded in the kind of fog that looks as if it can be cut into slices with a knife and served on a pie plate. Unfamiliar with the property, I found myself disoriented in the featureless sea of corn stalks and alfalfa fields surrounding the little pond. My confusion hardly mattered from a practical standpoint, but I've always been the kind of outdoorsman who likes to know which way north lies even when I don't need to.

Our party was unusually large that day, including Mike Kinney, our host, and Will Bailey, a friend of his from Alaska, in addition to Lori, my father, and our old friend Michael Crowder. I'd never hunted before with Mike or Will, but by the time we finished distributing the blocks around the pond they both felt like old friends. Good thing. With Cutter, Mike's eight year-old yellow Lab, at one end of the pit and Rocky at the other, we certainly had a full blind.

As we settled into place Michael expressed his dislike for hunting ducks in heavy fog, which he felt kept the birds from flying. I countered with an opposing opinion, based on nothing more than anecdotal memories of a few great hunts that took place on foggy mornings. Nonetheless, I had to admit that Michael had a point. Ducks can't fly in instrument conditions; they require visual orientation to the horizon. Fortunately, a chorus of feeding chuckles interrupted this discussion before it became too bogged down in abstract theory. The birds sounded as if they were straight overhead above the fog layer. "See," Michael said. "They can't spot our decoys!"

Fog has always occupied a spooky corner of the human imagination. Carl Sandburg claimed that it comes on little cats' feet and sits on silent haunches. Bram Stoker's Dracula could turn himself into fog at will, and no cinematic treatment of Sherlock Holmes or Jack the Ripper would be complete without invoking London's infamous version of the stuff. Perhaps most famously, the military theorist Carl von Clausewitz used fog as a metaphor for the confusion that reigns when armies join in battle, making discipline and strategy evaporate. Little did he know that the same principle applies in duck blinds, especially when multiple hunters and dogs unfamiliar with each other find themselves faced with a whole lot of ducks.

As we certainly did over the course of the morning, only to be plagued by a problem I'd like to experience more often: an excess of sportsmanship and good manners. Arriving in flocks of 15 to 20, the mallards—all prime northern greenheads newly arrived ahead of a brewing winter storm—circled our spread repeatedly at the edge of shotgun range without committing to land. No one wanted to be the first to stand and risk shooting prematurely, especially since the flat light made distinguishing drakes from hens more difficult than usual. And when a drake or two would break out of formation and settle in, everyone politely deferred to everyone else until the birds smelled a rat and flared back into the gloom. We managed to enjoy the spectacle the first several flocks provided without firing a shot.

By that time it had become clear that despite what looked like an excellent setup we weren't going to have dozens of birds backpeddling in our faces, and I suggested that the next time someone had a positive ID on a drake in range, they should call the shot and take it. Leave it to feminine common sense to show the way. The next time a lone drake peeled out of a circling flock to buzz the decoys, Lori simply stood up and crumpled it. "Someone had to break the ice," she explained as she reloaded.

We were obviously set up in a prime location. Flying above the fog layer, the birds were traveling from the north to feed in fields farther south, and even though we heard a lot of birds we couldn't see, enough descended and circled our spread to provide steady shooting. Abundant witnesses can make even a crack shot come a cropper, but the shooting itself wasn't a problem for any of us that day. Rather, it was the decision to stand and take the shots as they arose that proved difficult, as everyone kept being so damn polite.

But with Lori leading the way, we finally began to ignore the circling birds overhead and take the drakes in ones and twos as opportunities arose, at which point it became time for the dogs to join the pleasantly confused comedy. One of Thomas's Laws (and there are many) holds that experienced dogs will always reserve their most undisciplined performances for the maximum number of witnesses, and sure enough. Although I'd never hunted with Cutter before, she was by all accounts an experienced and highly capable retriever. Nonetheless, she lost the line on the first several falls, obligating Mike to wade out into the marsh and show us that he actually handled quite well himself.

Because of the dugout blind's low profile a breaking dog could easily wind up in the line of fire, and Mike had wisely fitted the dog box on each end with a permanently fixed leash to prevent a disaster. I'd kept Rocky on his leash after the first several falls, but when we finally put three greenheads down on the water at once, I sent him toward a bird on the opposite end of the pond from Cutter, providing him with a splendid opportunity to demonstrate Thomas's Law in action. As Cutter churned back toward shore with the first duck in her mouth, Rocky veered off line and took the bird away from her. I'd seen him pull this obnoxious stunt before, but thought I'd broken him of the habit on the lawn with the help of Kenai, a bucketful of dummies, and my e-collar. Unfortunately, the excitement and confusion that morning produced a classical case of behavioral regression. With apologies to all, I gave the bird back to its rightful owner and snapped Rocky's leash back on.

In fact, I've seen this scenario played out countless times before: experienced hunters and dogs in a crowded blind making rookie mistakes none of them would make if they were hunting in less confusing circumstances. As long as no one violates principles of safety (and no one came close to this one unforgivable sin that foggy morning), those mistakes usually wind up as nothing more than the subject of jokes at the end of the day (and I can only hope that they don't all come at my expense). Even so, it's nice to avoid them if possible, and over the years I've had enough experience with these situations to offer a few simple suggestions.

The hunters' immediate responsibility is to select a jagermeister to call the shots and then to support whatever decisions he or she makes. No need to draw out the selection process like a presidential election; if the choice doesn't obviously fall to the host or the most experienced member of the party, draw straws and be done with it. Faced with a circling flock of mallards or an inbound line of honkers, no thoughtful sportsman wants to risk discourtesy to other members of the party by standing up and shooting at the wrong time... when the birds are still at marginal range, say, or when a flock of twenty birds has set its wings to follow the single you just killed into the decoys. Unfortunately, the default position is usually a state of paralysis in which everyone defers to everyone else and no one shoots anything.

It's not necessary for the hunt master to be right every time. We've all made just the kind of mistakes mentioned above. It is necessary to communicate decisions clearly and effectively. "I think they might be in range on this pass," doesn't cut it. "Take 'em!" does. That's just the kind of decisive countermeasure von Clausewitz had in mind when he lamented the paralyzing effect of engagement over a century ago.

The dogs will likely need that kind of discipline even more than we will. Another of Thomas's Laws holds that the potential for canine confusion varies arithmetically with the number of guns in the blind and exponentially with the number of dogs, which is why bad performances by the dogs occur so frequently in front of witnesses. This is especially true of dogs that don't customarily share blinds with lots of company (like mine). When multiple guns start going off, birds are hitting the water, and other dogs are plunging in after them to a chorus of commands from several handlers, even the best trained dogs can lose their bearings.

After two hours of shooting, the fog of war inside the blind had burned off even if the fog overhead had not. We were taking the shots that needed taking and killing what we shot at cleanly. The only hen that fell was a single Lori dropped with two of us whispering "drake!" in her ears. The dogs were minding their manners and doing their job in capable if not quite stellar fashion (although Cutter did a superb job of running down a rare long cripple). Our only unrecovered birds turned out to be a mallard we never could account for and a green-wing I dumped in heavy cover while I was out of the blind without a dog. We had all learned to function together as a team.

And at the end of the day, that's the one enduring solution to the problem of confusion in the duck blind, just as it is whenever individuals must pool and coordinate their resources to attain any common goal, on the battlefield, the basketball court, or anywhere else in life. I can't think of a better setting to face that kind of challenge then a duck blind, surrounded by family, friends, and retrievers.

Texas hospitality: Lori tackles grilled snow goose.

CHAPTER SIXTY

Shaken,
Not Stirred

ONCE AGAIN, I credit my upbringing for the passion I feel for an element of the waterfowling experience that sometimes receives short shrift in the conventional outdoor literature.

My father always believed in eating what we shot, and he practiced that belief with conviction. When I was growing up, that sometimes meant spending what felt like hours searching for a fallen bird, and woe to the hunting partner who left a deer liver behind in the woods.

And it wasn't enough to eat our bag; we had to eat it right. He timed the hanging of the birds on the outside porch like a vintner babysitting casks of fine wine, and we always dressed out every inch of them, right down to the wingtips and drumsticks. Needless to say, ducks were always plucked, not skinned, a practice I've adhered to right into my own middle age.

"Aw, just skin 'em and breast 'em," I once heard one colleague advise a novice duck hunter as I hurried out of the hospital on my way to go hunting. Utter heresy, of course, and despite my date with the mallards I skidded to a halt and delivered a brief sermon on the subject. No one argued back, probably because it's impossible to argue with anyone speaking with the kind of conviction I felt.

There are practical reasons to cook ducks with their skins intact that go beyond the force of personal habit. Waterfowl cookery is tricky business, and the difference between a plump, juicy mallard and its desiccated, over-cooked counterpart can make it difficult to appreciate that one is eating representatives of the same species. While many factors contribute to the joy of a properly cooked duck, leaving the skin intact is one of the easiest ways to help insure a tender, savory result. Fresh from the oven, plucked ducks look especially appetizing on a serving platter, with their surfaces glazed and brilliant. And nothing compliments the texture of moist duck breast quite like a crisp morsel of skin.

In fairness, one can also make culinary arguments in favor of skinning. Duck skin is rich in fat, which may be of theoretical significance to those on restricted diets. This also means that a duck's skin contains many of the fat-soluble intangibles that contribute to flavor, including the bottom-of-the-sea taste of some marine species. I do skin sea ducks when I plan to cut them up rather than serve them whole, but I always offer a silent apology to the bird (and my father) when I do.

The main argument in favor of skinning ducks is that plucking them is a lot of work, but that's probably the least defensible of all. Granted, confronting a limit of big northern mallards and baring your thumb and forefinger to pluck them on a frigid December morning can be daunting. The trick is to regard the plucking as a labor of love, which always helps, at least for a little while.

Plucking machines can ease the burden, but good ones are cumbersome and pricey for personal use outside a hunting club. I prefer to begin my plucking chores while I'm still out in the blind. The task seems less intimidating approached one or two birds at a time, and nothing seems to draw ducks into decoys on slow mornings quite like distraction by other projects. Of course, this practice usually leaves the blind's occupants, canine and human, looking as if they've been tarred and feathered, but duck down always seems to disappear somehow if you tromp through the brush long enough.

Practical considerations aside, I admit feeling a certain automatic kinship with others who share my feelings on the value of plucking ducks, just as I do with hunters willing to make room for a wet dog beside them on a bench seat or hold their fire for a moment to appreciate an aerial display from a flock of pintails. These choices all reflect what once passed without irony as good taste. James Bond's famous dictum on the proper preparation of a martini may have seemed like an affectation at first, but it really reflected an appreciation for the finer things in life and a willingness to invest the extra effort necessary to experience them.

The afternoon after my impromptu lecture on the virtue of plucking ducks, I set up on a spring-fed slough to await the first northern mallards of the year. A sudden cold snap had filled the valley with birds, and when they finally returned from the fields the dog and I found ourselves too busy to think about anything but shooting and fetching. But when that part was over, I removed my gloves and began to pluck while Rocky sat beside me and licked feathers from the air.

Shaken, not stirred? Let's make that plucked, not skinned. The birds deserve it.

Don, Rocky, and Alaska guiding partner Ernie Holland beside a Montana slough.

Chapter Sixty-one

A Sociable Endeavor

A HIGH, THIN CLOUD LAYER occupied the sky, muting the afternoon light without obliterating it. As the flock of mallards circled the spread for the third time, we could see sunshine flashing from cupped primaries, but neither of us yielded to the temptation to stand and shoot. When a single drake peeled away from the flock and floated into the spread moments later, no one moved. The next pass justified our patience, and as a dozen birds finally extended their legs and committed to land, we rose simultaneously. With ducks flaring in all directions, Dick isolated two drakes on his side of the blind as I did the same on mine, and then it was time for the dogs to go to work. Remarkably, while this exercise required considerable coordination, neither of us had spoken a word.

I've always considered big game hunting a solitary sport, and most upland shooting affords generous space between participants. But while I've shot my share of ducks with no company other than a Labrador retriever, waterfowling also allows considerable opportunity to share time with other hunters in the field. Credit the way the game is played, for the relative confinement of a duck blind lends itself to polite conversation and philosophical discourse like few other outdoor venues. Of course, bad company in a duck blind, like bad company inside a snowbound cabin or aboard a small boat, can prove excruciating. But experienced hands learn to avoid such entrapments the way seasoned dogs avoid snakes, and the rewards of good company more than compensate for the occasional lapses that befall us all.

What defines good company in a duck blind? Certain fundamentals require no elaboration: the safe handling of firearms, sportsmanlike conduct, and regard for the game. But within these broad parameters considerable latitude prevails, and my personal short list of favorite duck blind companions draws from a wide spectrum of resources.

Personal experience and tradition count heavily. I always enjoy hunting with my parents because a morning spent in a blind with them invariably recalls odd snippets of memory from a very happy childhood. Ditto for a handful of old friends, some of whom I rarely see more than once a season. When we do get together, it's almost always by way of some outdoor activity, none of which affords a better opportunity to reminisce and catch up on interval developments in our lives. As seasons pass, it's always reassuring to discover how much you still have in common with the people who really matter.

While Lori honestly prefers fly rods and longbows to shotguns, that hasn't stopped us from enjoying time together in the duck blind. Even the best days of duck hunting involve remarkably little actual shooting as measured by the clock, and when I'm occupied with the shotgun she always manages to stay busy with the camera or the dog. Between appearances by the ducks, we find the isolation and solitude of the blind an ideal setting to reflect upon countless subjects that easily elude busy married couples during ordinary working days. Given today's strange standards of political correctness, I doubt we'll ever be invited to appear on any daytime TV talk shows to explain this inspired path to marital bliss, but you never know.

Then there are those hunting companions whose company you savor just because they love the whole process every bit as much as you do, a category that may prove the most exclusive of all. In a world in which an ever-increasing number of people Just Don't Get It, I find this kind of companionship quietly affirming, a form of reassurance that I am not alone in the appreciation of the values I deem important. While members of this inner circle invariably demonstrate certain measures of skill, the value of their company goes beyond the ability to shoot well or distinguish hen pintails from gadwalls in marginal light. Their presence enhances the ambience inside the blind simply because they know enough to care, about everything from the spectacle of the birds overhead to the importance of doing things right.

And while the duck blind offers plenty of opportunity for conversation, members of this select group often declare their credentials by what they leave unsaid. Hunt with a good hunter long enough and the two of you will just know somehow: when to rise and when to wait for another pass, which birds each of you should take from a flaring flock, whose dog gets to make the retrieve and whose has to remain on the bench. That's how the highest forms of human cooperation often become the simplest.

Just ask any duck hunter.

Lori and Rocky, set up for geese.

CHAPTER SIXTY-TWO

Amber Waves

FEW PLACES ON EARTH FEEL AS LONELY as a prairie stubble field during the darkness before dawn. Because farmers raise grain in open spaces, the sky overhead always feels enormous, especially on crisp, clear autumn mornings when the stars seem determined to remind us of our own insignificance in the cosmos. Absent terrain features to provide a lee, the wind stings harder than usual. And since each row of harvested wheat or barley looks identical to the rest, it's hard to avoid the monotony of the ground level surroundings when sunlight finally begins to spill over the distant horizon. From an aesthetic standpoint setting up in a grain field has little to recommend it, especially in contrast to the busy hum of wildlife activity that takes place near open water.

Which is why the justification for all our effort that morning depended on the birds and the shooting rather than the scenery, a leap of faith compounded by the lack of any guarantee that the geese would arrive at all. Set out a decoy spread in a pond or pothole and wait long enough and you'll always almost see something, even if it isn't waves of northern mallards. Grain field shoots, on the other hand, tend to be feast or famine affairs, and if the birds decide that another field looks better than the one you've chosen, you may be left with nothing but leftovers from the wheat harvest to contemplate for your trouble.

All of which explains why I spend almost all of my waterfowl hunting time over water. A precise set of circumstances must be in effect in order for me to change my mind, and that usually includes geese. My scouting must leave me convinced that against all odds the birds will actually arrive, even though I realize intellectually that there are never any guarantees. Above all, I must be able to entice several reliable friends into joining me, since misery loves company and nothing in the outdoor world produces misery like a huge decoy spread in a frozen field that all the birds have chosen to ignore.

After giving our setup the final seal of approval, I whistled to the dog and crawled into my coffin blind with Lori on one side and our old friend Jeff on the other and tried to think about somewhere warm while we waited for the moment of reckoning.

Ducks and geese are called waterfowl with good reason. Their dependence on water defines their character as well as their habitat and distinguishes them from all other game birds. As a young hunter, I quickly appreciated the significance of this association. Grouse and woodcock, at least to my naïve eye, could theoretically be anywhere. Ducks, on the other hand, were by nature limited to the tiny fraction of our surroundings occupied by open water, and I liked those odds. While killing limits became less important to me as I matured, I never lost my fascination for the wetlands ducks call home and rarely hunted them anywhere else.

But the lure of good field shooting eventually found ways to entice me. While I've killed plenty of mallards in stubble fields by now, the challenge of serious geese lies at the heart of the matter. Here on the prairie, fields are the place to make geese happen, for reasons both practical and altruistic. A goose shoot on the birds' home water may provide a memorable morning at the cost of driving the birds out of the county for the rest of the season. Stick to shooting the same birds in the fields where they're feeding and you can enjoy them as long as you can stand it.

Field shoots involve a lot more production than a trip to the nearest pothole for a limit of ducks. In the middle of that sea of stubble, it takes a lot of decoys to attract attention. Blinds must be more sophisticated than anything required near water surrounded by cover, and eventually that requires choosing among unpleasant alternatives: pit binds (work, cold ground), coffin blinds (miserable to shoot from, cold ground) and anything else (ineffective… and probably subject to the same cold ground anyway.)

But sometimes you just do what you have to do. It helps to think of this process as accepting a challenge.

By two hours after sunrise, we were all out of our blinds stamping our feet miserably against the chill. We hadn't seen or heard a bird all morning. Suddenly Lori, whose ears have not endured as many years of exposure to shotguns as mine, announced that she heard honkers to the north. Moments later, long lines of birds appeared against the distant sky, sending us scampering to ground like vampires at sunrise.

Cold? Tedium? Not any more.

Lori at 20-below, questioning her choice of marriage partners.

CHAPTER SIXTY-THREE

Deep Freeze

WHEN A FALLING THERMOMETER passes 20-below, the whole character of the outside world changes. Oddly enough, it's not the way things feel that first demands attention, but the way they sound. Simple acoustics explain the phenomenon: cold, dense air transmits sound more efficiently than its room temperature counterpart. But rational explanations have their limits, and this morning it's hard not to sense magic in the perfect clarity of a coyote's cry from the ridge beyond the creek or the pistol-shot pop of an ice-laden branch yielding to its burden.

Setting out decoys on a morning like this requires deliberate commitment, like crawling out of a warm sleeping bag or asking someone to marry you. It would just be so much easier to forget the whole thing, or at least put it off until later. But after enduring the alarm clock's rude blast and the long slog through the snow with the decoy bag balanced awkwardly over one shoulder, turning back seems even more ridiculous than persevering. Arranging the blocks neatly along the bank where I can reach them with a minimum of fumbling, I steel myself for the task and wade into the current.

A few seasons back, Sonny would have jumped right in beside

me. But experience has generated a measure of canine wisdom. He still loves the water as much as always, but on mornings like this he's happy to reserve his creek time for the ducks. Silhouetted against the snow in the eerie pre-dawn light, he sits and watches as I work, silent except for the tinkle of tags against the metal nameplate on his collar as he shivers. But when I climb back up the bank at last, he takes a few puppyish turns through the snow as if to suggest the completed spread is something we've done together. I see no reason to argue. His turn will come.

Waiting has become a lost art in our society. We've practically institutionalized its avoidance. The trick is to value the wait as much as what you're waiting for, an approach that admittedly goes better when your breath isn't turning to ice on your beard. But even on a morning like this it can be done, and these are the rewards: the crunch of hoofs on snow as a doe and fawn make their way back to the bedding cover, the warm feel of the dog against my leg as we huddle together on the downed log, the first rays of sunlight making the frosty brush along the banks glow like shattered crystal.

And finally, the ducks. Appropriately enough, we hear them long before we see them as rich throaty chuckles roll in like surf from the dark quadrant of the sky. The first wave passes high without giving us a second look, but then the sound of extended primaries tearing through the air fills my ears. Fumbling at the safety with my gloved thumb, I force myself to remain motionless and look down, but the racket builds until I just can't stand it any longer. Expecting half the ducks in the valley overhead, I straighten in time to see a mere half-dozen mallards spiraling down through the tops of the cottonwoods.

So much noise, so few ducks. The little flock looks like some kind of joke. But it's too cold to laugh, and with sunlight playing off the drakes' iridescent green heads it's time to stop being a spectator. Moments later, two birds lie kicking in the current as Sonny sets out to do what Labs do best. The retrieving turns out to be as easy as the shooting and both birds have already started to turn into feathered blocks of ice at my feet by the time the dog settles back into position beside me.

[284]

How cold is too cold for a Labrador retriever? I don't know and I'm not sure I want to. Over the years I've learned that I'm really the mineshaft canary for the dogs. If I can still stand it, they'll be just fine. If Sonny has a problem with his job description this morning, he's certainly keeping it to himself. Even with ice tracing a pale, delicate pattern upon his whiskers, he looks ready for the next set, and fifteen minutes later he gets his wish.

Hunting spring-fed creeks, frigid weather means fast shooting and that part is over all too quickly. The dog and I have done well together this morning (five shots, five drakes in the game vest) and there is always satisfaction to be found in such quiet efficiency. But as I pack to leave I realize I will remember what I saw and heard even more than what I shot. We have experienced a glimpse of the world others can only imagine. Such is the spell of special times in special places: the places where the ducks live.

The gun room at our friend Dick Negley's Gulf Coast property.

CHAPTER SIXTY-FOUR

Best Guns

SOMEHOW I'VE MANAGED to fill the back page of *Ducks Unlimited* for years with hardly a word on the subject of firearms, even though good shotguns are obviously a central element of the duck hunting experience. This omission makes me something of an anomaly among wing-shooting writers, who as a group never seem to run out of things to say about chokes and barrels, topics that at least spare them the necessity of getting up in the dark and shivering in the rain. My own aversion to technical gun talk derives largely from a preference for other subject matter, especially wildlife, a source of endless fascination, and retrievers, which if nothing else can be counted on to lick your face at the end of a long day in the field. No one has yet made a shotgun capable of offering such solace.

But I also regard wing-shooting as more art than science and have always bridled at the application of technical analysis to subjects that don't warrant it. Years ago when I was learning to shoot, an old, retired market hunter used to haunt our local skeet range. A fantastic shot, he supplemented his Social Security check by dealing in used guns. Whenever someone was having a particularly bad day, he would suggest that a gun with, say, a bit more drop at heel would likely solve the problem. Inevitably, he would have just such a gun in the back of his car. He would then proceed to demonstrate its virtues with some nifty display of trick shooting. He sold a lot of guns that way, but even as a kid it didn't take me long to learn the essential lesson. Great shots can shoot well with almost anything and, alas, vice versa.

While I enjoy good guns and can certainly appreciate the difference between a Parker and whatever is gathering dust at the local hardware store, I've never been convinced that spending more money on a shotgun will translate into more birds with fewer shells at the end of the day. Furthermore, duck blinds are not necessarily good places for good guns. All serious waterfowl hunting eventually requires shotguns to cross the arbitrary line between use and abuse, especially when the hunting takes place over salt water. That's a lot to ask of a shotgun whose craftsmanship challenges the distinction between utility and art.

No venue illustrates this dilemma like Alaska, where a simple limit of ducks often means camping in the rain and dragging guns and gear through miles of tidal mud. I could never bring myself to do that to a shotgun that looked as if it belonged on a magazine cover. As much as I enjoy doubles, when I lived up north my standard Alaska duck gun was an old pump that looked like a prosecution exhibit in a liquor store robbery trial. It wasn't going to win any beauty contests and I never did become completely comfortable with its awkward balance and sloppy action. But it proved perfectly capable of knocking sea ducks out of the sky, and loaded with slugs it made a formidable bear defense gun in camp. I can't count the nights I spent in a tent on Kodiak Island or the shores of Cook Inlet sleeping comfortably just because that old beater was lying within easy reach of my sleeping bag. I always assumed I would drop the gun overboard someday without shedding a tear, but it's still resting in the closet of our Alaska home, pitted and rusty but ready to serve, probably for more seasons than I am.

A century of waterfowling tradition has produced plenty of conventional wisdom concerning the selection of duck guns that, as usual, proves more conventional than wise. Robert Ruark once advised to use enough gun, but in the case of puddle ducks at least I think we've generally overdone it. Most of my local duck hunting nowadays takes place over decoys at close range where I am perfectly happy with open chokes, short barrels, and 20 gauges. The key, as in all shooting sports, is to know your range and stick to it. As with the selection of equipment for all manner of outdoor pursuits, what works best is what works for you.

So with apologies to my old friend Steve Bodio, who parlayed the term into not just one book title but two, I offer my own blue-collar definition of a best gun. It's the one you happen to be holding in your hand at the time. Accepting this concept leaves you free to concentrate on what really counts: the dogs, the company, and above all the birds and the places they call home.

Set up for mallards on Kodiak.

CHAPTER SIXTY-FIVE

Duck Soup

WHEN THE BIRDS CAME BARRELING IN LOW over the top of the reeds at the far end of the pothole, I recognized them immediately as blue-wings. Because they depart so much earlier than all the rest of our local puddle ducks we rarely get to shoot them here, even on opening day. I thumbed my safety back and forth eagerly as they roared across the pond. "Don't miss!" I instructed myself, which is probably why the first shot of the new season went awry. Fortunately I settled down with my second barrel, and there were still plenty of blue-wings around. By the end of the morning a limit of teal was hanging from my duck strap, thanks to some improved shooting on my part and a strong performance from old Sky, still the best Lab ever to occupy our kennel.

Blue-wings are gorgeous little birds and their erratic, high speed flight patterns offer challenging gunning, but my enthusiasm for teal that morning had a more practical basis: I love to eat them. Some hunters consider all ducks the same on the table, which is like regarding all bottles of wine as equivalent whether the vintage is a Premier Grand Cru or a fortified grape juice poured from a box. To appreciate duck cookery you have to know its raw ingredients. Prime, grain fattened mallards serve as an appropriate benchmark, but I personally prefer blue-wings and pintails because of their succulence and the fine grain of their meat. At the other end of the spectrum shovelers, gadwalls, and sea ducks are all perfectly edible, although they go best with some imagination invested in their cooking. The best of the lot require no embellishment. My favorite approach to blue-wings is to hang them, roast them, and eat them unadorned with anything more than salt and pepper. Save the barbecue sauce for the goldeneyes.

I'm always dismayed by the number of hunters who just don't like to eat ducks, especially since I've been gnawing my way through them enthusiastically ever since I graduated to solid food. Some of the unappreciative among us grind their birds into burger or dry the meat into jerky, while others give them away to friends who know better or are too polite to refuse. Too bad; the hunting experience is never as complete as when you cook and eat what you've shot yourself.

Some of us just aren't going to enjoy eating ducks the same way I don't enjoy eating beets, in which case there isn't much to be done about it. But aversion to wild duck on the table often arises from failure in the kitchen. No game suffers a more uneven culinary reputation, and it cannot be an accident that no wild fowl is easier to cook improperly. It really isn't the birds' fault. On countless occasions I've served ducks to hunting friends who expressed no enthusiasm initially only to have them leave eager for more.

While I can't tell anyone how to cook ducks in a thousand words, it's easy to identify the commonest error: over-cooking, the culprit in most cases of wild game mismanagement in the kitchen. I don't know what it is about ducks that invites cooks to expose them to twice the heat that's good for them. Duck changes character completely somewhere between rare and well done and the difference is as profound as the contrast between *maguro* at a sushi bar and canned tuna in a brown bag sandwich. When I've started with one of the prime specimens mentioned earlier, I think of duck as good beef and aim for an end result the color and consistency of rare tenderloin. If your cooked duck looks gray and leathery when you cut into it, you've overdone it. I wouldn't like it either.

[292]

The approach to duck cookery can certainly vary with the circumstances. The cooking facilities in our old Cook Inlet duck shack consisted of a single two-burner Coleman stove. Roasting ducks was impossible. Most nights we had to settle for duck soup made from whatever we'd shot that morning combined with rain soaked leftovers and assorted canned goods. The simmering soup pot always filled the little plywood shack with the most savory smells imaginable no matter what its contents. More often than not the finished product tasted faintly of white gas, but no one ever objected. If you're having trouble making someone a believer, serve them duck soup piping hot in a tiny cabin rocked by wind, with rain pelting overhead on a tin roof and a wet retriever or two underfoot. I can practically guarantee conversion.

Alaska camp cookery wasn't always that desperate. Our friend Bob May has a real kitchen in his cabin, and when we'd gather there for late season duck hunts it was a busy place after hours. Shooting light doesn't last long on Kodiak Island in December, and elaborate duck cookery helped occupy the long winter nights. The bag was mostly sea ducks but they all tasted good, especially after a few glasses of wine.

Of course taste is an individual matter, and I wouldn't presume to tell anyone what to like or disdain on the table. But making an honest effort to get it right is good for all of us, and good for duck hunting. Surveys consistently show that a large majority of America's non-hunting public approves of hunting when hunters eat what they shoot. Those numbers plummet dramatically when we're perceived as hunting primarily for trophies or "sport". Sending a dozen hastily cleaned mallards off to an uncertain fate at a neighbor's house isn't a crime like chopping the antlers off a bull elk and leaving the meat to rot, but it all adds up in the end. The more we take responsibility for cooking and eating what we shoot at the end of the day, the more rewarding duck hunting becomes for all of us.

Teal decoys done for the day.

CHAPTER SIXTY-SIX

The Art of Deception

THE MOMENT THE FLOCK APPEARED against the lead gray sky, we knew they were ours. Although they were still a quarter mile out, they'd already started to cup their wings and descend and an electronic guidance system couldn't have provided them a straighter path to our decoys. Even with their flaps down, mallards can cover a hundred yards in short order and by the time we'd hushed the dogs and shifted into shooting position it was time to take them. As the dogs hit the water and began to churn their way toward the birds kicking in the decoys, I had to marvel at the simplicity of it all: a strategic plan executed to perfection courtesy of nothing more elaborate than a dozen phony mallards resting on the water.

Given the wealth of stuff the catalogs tell us we need to shoot ducks nowadays, it's instructive to realize how recently we got along with so little. Decoys, however, have been an essential part of the waterfowler's armamentarium right from the beginning… longer than shotguns, in fact. Archeological digs have recovered well preserved reed decoys Native American hunters used to lure ducks into range over 2000 years ago. Since they were hunting with bows and nets, those simple blocks must have been convincing even though they look crude by moderns standards. Of course, human opinions were never the ones that counted.

The development of the decoy carver's craft along our Eastern seaboard during the post-Colonial era requires little introduction. Today, antique decoys are widely hailed as examples of American folk art. That term immediately arouses my suspicions, since it implies that sculptors on the Eastern Shore of Maryland were doing something qualitatively different than sculptors in European studios, and I don't appreciate the condescension. In this case however, the distinction may enjoy some validity. Early American decoy carvers were largely inspired by market driven need to kill more birds. Their work's visual appeal depended heavily on the function-is-beauty school of esthetics, while the world recognized those wooden canvasbacks and redheads as *objets d'art* largely after the fact.

Judged by modern standards of realism, those early carvings didn't always look much like ducks. Many invoked a frontier version of Impressionism, which was coincidentally emerging as an artistic genre in the salons of Paris around the same time. Graceful silhouettes suggested waterfowl more than they imitated them, and the markings on many early wooden decoys remind me of Roger Tory Petersen's nearly schematic representations in his Field Guide series. But while final artistic judgments would have to await the passage of time, those carved decoys must have appealed to their intended contemporary audience: the waterfowl of the Atlantic Flyway. Market hunters just didn't have time to indulge in art for art's sake.

The explosion of synthetics technology that followed the end of the Second World War influenced virtually every aspect of American life including our decoy spreads. Suddenly it became possible to mass-produce decoys that actually looked like ducks. Foam and plastic provided the substrate for details impossible for carvers to achieve, at least on a commercial scale. Colors looked bright and stayed bright. And duck decoys, like Detroit automobiles, became uniform, devoid of individual variation within a batch.

Fellow romantics will probably sense where this argument is

headed, but before we follow it there let's give progress its due. Modern decoys in all their incarnations have plenty to recommend them on practical grounds. They are light, compact, and generally durable (with considerable variation in this last variable by model). Setting out to tromp across two miles of tidal mud in the dark, I can think of no easier way to make a puddle look inviting to ducks than a pack full of collapsible rubber decoys. And yes, I have dozens of variations on the theme squirreled away in corners of the barn, ready to be dusted off and put to good use next fall.

But a hundred years from now, no one is going to present any of them to the world as examples of art, folk or otherwise. Interestingly, the most important lessons classical decoy carving has to teach us may not concern esthetics but the manner in which old decoys attracted ducks. While modern versions often strive for absolute realism, traditional masters recognized that suggestion and impression counted more than minute details. What matters is not how much the decoy looks like a duck to us when it's resting in our hands, but how much it looks like a duck to a flock of mallards a hundred yards away on a rainy, gray morning.

Blurring the distinction between illusion and reality has been part of our craft since the first Paleolithic hunter tied a bundle of reeds together and tossed it out on a pond. Sometimes the surest route forward comes through studying these lessons of the past.

Texas teal.

CHAPTER SIXTY-SEVEN

Shooting Nothing

UNSEASONABLY WARM WEATHER made migrating birds hold up north of the border through mid-November that year. Bows and arrows kept me busy in the woods even after two rounds of visiting pheasant hunters had been and gone, but the Labs seemed to know we should have been hunting ducks. They were starting to act neglected, as if these developments were my fault instead of nature's, and when the first honest storm of the season dumped two feet of snow on the ground I greeted the sight with relief.

That afternoon the sky was full of southbound honkers and waves of northern greenheads. After dinner, I called one of my hunting partners and made plans for the following morning. The frenzy of excitement that greeted me when I walked out to the kennel in the dark made the brisk wind chill factor more tolerable. Enthusiasm means as much as a good nose in a working retriever, and that morning the boys greeted me with a double dose of desire.

We arrived at the slough a few minutes later than planned. A flock of mallards tried to land on Jim's head as we were setting out the decoys. "They'll be back," I assured him as we put the finishing touches on the spread and stomped out a blind in the snow-laden willows. Then we settled in to do what ambush hunters do best: wait.

The Labs remembered their manners and sat patiently studying the sky as if they'd just graduated from charm school. The southwest breeze began to freshen right after sunrise. Although that's usually our warmest winter wind, the temperature actually dropped once the sun cleared the horizon and the chill seemed to push through my woolens and into my bones. At least the breeze brought the decoys to life as they bobbed about in the open lead of water between the ice shelves lining the banks. Since Jim had never hunted there before, I assured him that the conditions were perfect and recounted stories of great shooting I'd enjoyed there on similar days. All we had to do was wait for flights of mallards to return from the fields to the only piece of open water for miles around.

Two hours later, the sole game bird we'd seen over the slough had been a lonely looking sharptail. My brash assurances began to lose their authority and even the Labs had started to fidget. The conditions may have been perfect, but our outing was beginning to look suspiciously like another confrontation with waterfowling's biggest challenge: shooting nothing.

As much as the admission pains me, I blame writers for creating the Grand Illusion: that most days in the field culminate in furious (and flawless) shooting, brilliant dog work, and bulging game vests. Veterans know that nothing could be further from the truth, but writers persist for one practical reason. It's easier to write a duck hunting story when the narrative actually contains some ducks.

Days spent shooting nothing break down into three categories. Some days, you shoot without hitting anything. (Of course, that has never, ever happened to me.) Then there are mornings when birds appear but never fly into shotgun range. Finally come the times that truly try men's souls: the days when you rise in the dark and shiver through elaborate preparations but never see a bird. Years ago, I dubbed those Rachel Carson Mornings in honor of the pioneering environmental activist who introduced us to the specter of a silent spring. Duck hunts like that can be grimly humorous, but the humor usually takes weeks or months to appreciate after those cold, lonely hours in the blind.

For waterfowlers, the concept reaches its fullest expression when geese are the quarry. The pain of striking out varies directly with the amount of effort expended, and skies never look as empty as they do after you've spent hours setting out hundreds of decoys in a frozen field the geese have decided to avoid. That happens more often than most of us care to admit, at least to rational, non-hunting family and friends.

Since I've experienced my share of days that produced no birds, I've developed my own coping mechanisms. Our cameras always go with us when Lori and I head to a duck blind, and on slow mornings we take pictures of whatever is at hand. (Note that no amount of calling skill can produce birds from a barren sky like getting out of the blind to photograph the dogs.) I get a surprising amount of "writing" done on slow mornings, even though it takes place between my ears rather than at the keyboard. And I try to choose hunting partners capable of sustained conversations on a variety of subjects.

But the most rewarding Silent Spring Mornings often take place when I'm enjoying no company other than the dogs'. Release from hunting's responsibilities (accurate identification of birds on the wing, getting the shot column to the right place at the right time) means freedom to observe the natural world without distraction. Perhaps my willingness to trade birds for imponderables simply means I'm getting older... or wiser.

Back at the ice rimmed slough, our supply of hunting stories was running low after two hours of conversation. My teeth were chattering and the stalwart Labs had curled up at my feet. "What do you think?" I finally asked Jim. I already knew what I thought.

"I'll stick it out as long as you want," he replied. That's the trouble with good hunting partners. They never let you off the hook.

But it was Thanksgiving, and our visiting kids provided a perfect excuse. I unloaded my shotgun and waded out toward the decoys. It was time to head home and become fathers and husbands again. I wished we'd shot some birds, but we'd enjoyed a morning free of taxes and terrorists and all the other ills that plague modern society.

Taken in context, shooting nothing doesn't feel at all like failure.

Iced up and frozen out; January in Montana.

CHAPTER SIXTY-EIGHT

Table for Two

THE LATE DUCK SEASON was slow around our place that year, thanks to an unusually bitter cold snap that convinced a lot of migrating mallards to overfly us. But the paucity of ducks only made me keener to enjoy those I could find, which is why I threw my waders and a bag of decoys into the back of the truck when Lori and I set out on an afternoon pheasant hunt last December. Of course the Labs didn't care whether we were hunting roosters or waterfowl, as long as we were hunting something.

The day was sunny but crisp with just enough breeze out of the north to make our faces smart as we followed old Rocky through the cattails. I had ice in my beard by the time we circled back to the rig carrying a brace of pheasants apiece, with a couple of sharptails thrown in for good measure. The wind's bite would have provided a perfect excuse to declare victory and retreat to the fireplace, but we'd seen a few small flocks of mallards trading up and down the valley and I suspected that some of them would return to the little spring-fed creek by sundown. "What do you think?" I asked my wife.

"I think I'd really like a duck dinner tonight," she replied. "Besides, Kenai deserves a chance to hunt too."

Lori had a point. Since Kenai, Rocky's son, tended to outrun the old man in the upland cover by then, I'd left him in the dog box during our bird hunt. Lori and Kenai have always enjoyed a special friendship, and despite the cold she wasn't about to leave for home without giving him a chance to perform.

Soon we were sitting beside a dozen decoys on a quiet backwater of the creek, scanning the skies, and stamping our feet against the chill as the sun descended toward the mountains behind us. That creek has provided me with some fast duck shooting over the years, but I'd already resigned myself to the probability of a quiet evening. Since the best way to confront reduced opportunity is with reduced expectations, I decided to concentrate on Lori's earlier request: a mallard dinner for two.

While I enjoy the exertion that upland bird hunting demands, powering through the cover behind an eager dog doesn't allow much opportunity to appreciate undisturbed wildlife. What you see is what you flush, illustrating a variation of the physicist's Heisenberg Uncertainty Principle: the very act of observing inevitably alters the nature of the observed. Sitting quietly beside a decoy spread is another matter. Even in December, with the landscape locked in snow and much of the local wildlife absent for the winter, the habitat around us came alive as soon as we sat still and let it. As we watched a marsh hawk work the cattails on silent wings, scarlet buffalo berries gleamed like rubies from the brush around us. Then a muskrat emerged from the water, crawled onto the ice shelf in front of us, and shook, transforming its waterlogged coat into a corona of delicate guard hairs. We might have forgotten all about the absent ducks at that point, save for our determination to put a pair of them on the table.

When the breeze finally dropped off near the end of shooting light, the still air rendered the decoys lifeless on the water. But it also created splendid acoustics that allowed me to hear a pair of mallards chuckling long before I caught sight of them above the cottonwoods to the west. By the time I dug my call out of my coat they'd already set their wings, and when they circled in front of us on final approach the oblique light offered me a definitive look at their plumage. "The drake's in the rear," I whispered to Lori. "Take him."

Did she ever. At the sound of the report from her 20-gauge, the bird folded midair. Its momentum still carried it back over our heads, where it fell into a particularly nasty tangle of cattails and willows. While Lori broke her shotgun, I stepped out of the brush, gave Kenai the line, and let him do what he'd been waiting to do all afternoon.

A delicate eater, Lori can make due with half a mallard... but I can't. A duck dinner has always meant just that to me: one whole duck resting on my plate, crisp on the outside, rare in the middle. So even with the temperature dropping and my toes beginning to tingle, I resolved to stick it out to the bitter end. The hands on my watch confirmed that the end would come soon enough, one way or another. And suddenly there it was, hanging right over the decoys, as another pair of mallards appeared from nowhere. "Take the drake!" I said to Lori, and when she rose I stood beside her, ready to provide a backup shot she didn't need. Moments later, Kenai completed what we'd set out to accomplish.

I worked for my ducks in Montana that season, but thanks to the hospitality of friends I also enjoyed my share of the epic waterfowling writers love to write about: in Washington's Columbia Basin, on the Texas Gulf Coast, and even in Argentina when I decided to trade my bow for a borrowed shotgun one memorable morning. But from the perspective of the season's end, I can't say that any of those hunts meant more than the quiet evenings I spent beside a simple decoy spread near home in the company of Lori and the dogs.

Especially when those evenings ended the way I never tire of them ending: at my own table, with Lori sitting across from me, a pair of roasted mallards between us on a platter, and Kenai and Rocky minding their manners on the floor but hoping something edible falls there by mistake while we make our plans for the day to come.

Daughter Gen shaking, not stirring.

CHAPTER SIXTY-NINE

101 Uses for a Dead Duck

One of the six cardinal principles of the North American Model of Wildlife Conservation reminds us that wildlife should not be taken without a valid reason. Food and self-defense top the list of generally accepted motivations for killing game, while reasonable people can and do argue about many of those that follow.

Despite a lifetime spent in wild places in the company of dangerous animals, including years spent working as a brown bear guide in Alaska, I've never had to kill any wild creature in self-defense, although I've come close several times. If I ever do, I doubt that the aggressor responsible for breaking this string of good luck will be a duck.

Game cookery and cuisine, as emphasized throughout this volume, offer all the justification any of us will ever need for killing ducks and geese. However, with a bit of imagination it's possible to discover or invent even more ways to utilize what we bring back from the duck blind. The satisfaction of doing so reflects the honorable tradition of utilizing by choice as much as possible from the game we kill, just as our hunter-gatherer forebears once did by necessity.

Since waterfowl are so inherently beautiful, the urge to preserve that beauty should come as no surprise. I'm not a collector and we don't have a lot of bird taxidermy in our home, but most of the mounted birds we do have are waterfowl: a can, a mottled duck, a harlequin, a paradise duck, a woody. Of note, the story behind each of those five specimens left a sufficient impression upon me to warrant inclusion in this book. When I come home after a rough shift at my medical day job, I can sit down in front of one of those preserved birds and experience immediate mental transportation back to the comforting ambience of a distant duck blind. Compared to the usual therapeutic alternatives for stress, mounted ducks are cheaper, more effective, and have fewer side effects.

Waterfowl taxidermy can serve purposes higher than personal enjoyment. On my initial visit to the home of longtime DU supporter Mark Pearce in Bozeman, Montana, I entered his shop prior to an early morning duck hunt and found myself face to face with a collection of every legal waterfowl in North America. What an opportunity to provide education and inspiration to a young hunter and potential advocate for waterfowl! If I were a kid, I could easily have spent an hour studying those mounted specimens, and since I still was a kid, at heart if not in fact, that's just what I did when we returned from the blind.

Some alternative uses for what comes home on the game strap turn out better than others. Years ago when I was living out on the prairie during a banner duck year, my sister-in-law decided she wanted to make everyone in the family wild duck down comforters for Christmas. We'd been eating ducks for breakfast, lunch, and dinner in order to keep the freezer's contents within legal possession limits, and I was tired of plucking ducks. Employing chicanery straight from Tom Sawyer, I allowed that I might be able to let her pluck some ducks and keep the down, but only if she presented the birds in perfect condition for the kitchen.

For the next month, I shot, she plucked, and everyone was happy. Then one night at dinner she proudly opened a box and presented the initial result of her labor to the gathering, and a truly lovely comforter it was. Unfortunately, she had neglected to address one crucial detail: the lice that love to call waterfowl home. When her down comforter began to buzz and wiggle before our eyes, she emitted a piercing shriek and begged my brother-in-law to haul her handiwork to the garbage can without delay. I plucked my own ducks for the rest of the season, and we all received jars of chokecherry jelly for Christmas.

The same factors that turn ordinarily rational people into duck hunters also turn many of them into fly-fishermen, and the fly-tying bench offers another alternative opportunity to utilize the waterfowl we take each season. While the development of new synthetic tying materials has revolutionized the art, I'm old enough to remember when my father's tying bench lay buried beneath a splendid pile of fur and feathers, most of which he'd obtained himself in the field. The classical fly-tying literature demonstrates abundant uses for wild duck feathers, and a growing retro movement in favor of natural materials among modern tiers has appropriately re-emphasized their utility and aesthetic appeal.

Fly tiers have been turning barred mallard flank feathers into faux mayfly wings for generations. Teal feathers make great nymph legs, and primaries from many species enjoy all kinds of uses at the tying bench. Even readers who don't tie flies, or fly-fish at all, can generate all kinds of goodwill by taking orders from friends who do at the beginning of each season. Nothing but a bit of effort to save what would otherwise be discarded is required, and this kind of thoughtfulness can only be good for duck hunters and duck hunting in the end.

Mounted ducks, dry flies, and down quilts (still not a bad idea, as long as the seamstress de-louses the raw materials appropriately before sewing) may seem little more than obscure end notes to the already rich and complex world of waterfowling, but they reflect important principles. Utilizing what we shoot should be as gratifying as the shooting, and the more complete the utilization, the more enduring the gratification. Furthermore, the non-hunting public that will ultimately determine the future of hunting is far more likely to approve of what we do if they know hunters are making full use of what they kill. Follow that logic to its conclusion and you'll find that nymph legs can actually be good for duck hunting.

And that in turn is actually good for ducks.

Closing time: sunset over the marsh.

CHAPTER SEVENTY

The Way
We Were

NO ONE EVER INTENDED my vintage Parker to spew steel shot, and because of the deleterious effects of modern waterfowl loads on those old, tightly choked barrels, I don't often take my one classic side by side duck hunting. But at least once every season, I yield to temptation. I know I won't kill any more birds with it. In fact, because of its relative unfamiliarity, I'll likely kill fewer. But the Parker has a way of grounding me in my own sense of history that's impossible to ignore.

I usually make this choice when I'm in a philosophical mood unsuited to the distractions of even the best human company, and so it is today. I've walked a lot farther out in the middle of nowhere than I had to, and Rocky serves as my only companion.

There's a certain universality to the process of waiting for shooting light in the middle of a duck marsh that transcends borders and dissolves conventional notions of place and setting. Lawrence Durrell concludes *Justine*, the first volume of his magnificent Alexandria Quartet, with a waterfowling scene unparalleled anywhere in English literature. The characters represent an eclectic mix of Egyptian Copts and dissolute British expatriates and the action takes place half a world away, but the prose resonates with the familiarity of anyone's last duck hunt. And just like Durrell's fictional shoot on the shores of Egypt's Lake Mareotis, the slow sunrise taking place before me, punctuated by the warm feel of the dog beside me on the bench and the slow crescendo of wings building overhead, could be happening anywhere.

And more to the point, at any time, at least within the last century's worth of North American waterfowling. Granted, my choice of firearms this morning deliberately emphasizes this connection to the past, but nothing important about duck hunting has really changed since the early chronicles of the sport. Even though they aren't hand-carved, the decoys bobbing gently on the surface of the pothole look like they came right out of a vintage sporting print. Rocky's genetics are essentially the same as his predecessors' a hundred years ago. The highballs, come-backs, and chuckles from my duck call belong on the Golden Oldies list. And that's about all there is to it.

All of which really becomes remarkable when one considers the pace of change that has taken place over the last century in other forms of outdoor sport. While regular duck hunting readers know me principally by way of my enthusiasm for shotguns and Labrador retrievers, I devote just as much time afield to the pursuit of big game (albeit with traditional wooden bows) and any fish willing to hit a fly. Fly-fishing and bowhunting have changed so much over the course of my lifetime that modern methods and techniques would practically be unrecognizable to enthusiasts a few generations removed. Credit (or blame) a combination of technology, improved communications, and an underlying streak of human laziness. But Aldo Leopold's prescient warnings about the impact of change for change's sake in the field have largely gone unheeded in the quest for more and bigger trout and deer.

But with only occasional exceptions, this worrisome impulse has hardly impacted the waterfowler's world at all. Duck hunters seem to relish an innate sense of their own history. They wear tattered hunting coats that should have been turned into kennel bedding years ago. They lug around old decoys faded by seasons worth of weather even though lighter, brighter replacements are only a trip to the nearest sporting goods store away. They drink coffee from leaky thermos bottles and blow calls with cracked reeds. All this because these means and methods have worked before, and they're smart enough to know that what isn't broke doesn't need fixing.

And yes, they shoot old shotguns just because the smell of the oil on the barrel and the feel of the stock against their cheek reminds them of their connection to other places and other times.

The trouble with duck blind philosophy is the ease with which it distracts the participant from the business at hand. All of a sudden it's shooting light and Rocky's eager whine draws my attention skyward, where a small flock of mallards has started to spiral down toward the blocks. A drake folds at my first barrel's report but, accustomed to my Browning, I fumble away an easy opportunity to complete the double. By the time my finger has found the Parker's elusive second trigger, the rest of the flock has reached marginal range and I hold my fire.

Perhaps the concept of voluntary restraint represents our generation's most significant contribution to the history of waterfowling. If so, we have no reason to be ashamed.

Below zero on a steaming Montana slough.

CHAPTER SEVENTY-ONE

The Big Chill

HERE IS HOW TO TELL when the ambient temperature in the blind has fallen below zero, even if you don't have a thermometer...

The water that splashed onto the decoys when you pitched them onto the spring-fed pond a minute ago has already turned to ice. The dog's muzzle sports a frosty corona of rime. The brass bases of the shotgun shells nip the exposed tips of your fingers as you load your gun. Your feet stamp the ground involuntarily, and the snow underfoot squeaks whenever you move. Distant sounds—a whitetail's alarm snort, a raven's playful croak—greet your ears with unnatural clarity. Above all, you hope that the ducks will arrive now, for camaraderie and appreciation of nature can only sustain you so long on mornings like this.

We'd confirmed all those criteria and more one December morning a few seasons back. My two companions in the blind represented the extremes in the spectrum of response to the cold. Even though shooting light was still fifteen minutes away, I had already started to feel sorry for Lori. An adventuresome woman, she can shrug off just about any form of adversity in the field with two exceptions: rattlesnakes and bitter cold. Despite multiple layers of wool, insulated boots, and pockets full of hand-warmers, she was already shivering. I tried to console her by telling her she was beautiful even when her nose was running, but somehow that compliment didn't produce its intended effect.

Then there was Rocky. With eight seasons of cold weather duck hunting behind him, he knew exactly why we were there. He couldn't have looked happier had he been sitting in front of the fireplace with a bone to chew. After a brief, puppyish romp through the snow, he'd settled in beside me on the bench in his customary duck blind posture: eyes trained skyward, head rotating slowly in search of birds, otherwise motionless and silent as a statue. I knew he'd be the last to vote in favor of leaving.

A pair of mallards suddenly appeared out of nowhere, filling the air with the shrill sound of setting wings before they fluttered down into the edge of the decoy spread. "Five more minutes," I whispered after a glance at my watch. Rocky shuddered silently beside me in an effort to contain his excitement.

Lori and I sat and waited.

While duck hunting is seldom considered a warm weather activity, extreme cold—at least as measured by the thermometer— isn't a common element of the experience, for logical reasons. Ducks need water, and when water is exposed to enough cold for enough time, it turns to ice. Sub-zero duck hunting requires a source of ice-resistant water. The sea is one, but since oceans naturally moderate air temperatures, truly frigid saltwater duck hunting opportunities don't arise that often, even on the coast of Alaska.

I once spent several mornings shivering beside a power station outflow pond on the Alberta prairie in minus-20 weather. We shot plenty of ducks, but the ambience felt artificial. Current stays open longer than still water, and I've spent my share of time huddled beside icy rivers trying to eke out one last limit at the end of the season. But those limits usually contained more goldeneyes than mallards, and I often had to quit early when floating ice began to pose a hazard to the dogs.

Which brings us to my favorite sub-zero waterfowl venue: spring-fed creeks and ponds on the high plains. When an aquifer reaches the surface at a constant temperature from a subterranean source, its issue can prove remarkably resistant to cold. Our local spring creek runs 26 miles from its source to its confluence with a tributary of the Missouri and I've never seen it frozen all the way across, even during severe, extended cold snaps. During the winter, every duck in the county knows the location of many smaller sources of open water, and so do I.

But when it comes to misery and outright hypothermia—the ultimate expression of the Big Chill—cold air temperatures aren't the biggest threat to comfort or survival. Wind and rain are the culprits, increasing the rate of heat loss from the body and compromising clothing's ability to insulate. Of course, wet, blustery weather creates classical duck hunting conditions as wind keeps birds moving and low ceilings force them to fly close to the deck, but wind and rain seldom accompany the Arctic highs that make the thermometer plunge to double-digits below. Paradoxically, hunters huddled in a marsh with horizontal rain lashing the blind, decoys bouncing on the waves, and the temperature just above freezing operate in conditions more likely to produce true hypothermia than those encountered beside a spring-fed pond in the dead of winter when it's 50 degrees colder.

Today's availability of innovative, high quality outdoor clothing makes enduring any of these harsh conditions easier than it was a generation ago. Hunters who outfit themselves wisely and adhere to the principle of dressing in layers—an inner wicking layer to conduct moisture away from the skin, an outer protective layer to repel wind and rain, and an insulating layer to prevent loss of body heat sandwiched between—can survive almost any duck hunting conditions.

But surviving a duck hunt and enjoying it are different matters.

Back at our blind, shooting light arrived uneventfully. Nothing increases the chill factor like empty skies, and by the time the sun's cold disc had cleared the horizon I was fantasizing about a hot breakfast back home. Then I felt Rocky pivot on the seat beside me, and suddenly a flock of mallards was breaking over the blind from behind us. "Take 'em!" I whispered unnecessarily just before Lori's shotgun barked, and then I was picking green heads of my own from the riot of wings.

The ability to enjoy duck hunting under challenging conditions doesn't come in a box. It requires enthusiasm, dedication, and patience. Of course, a sky full of ducks never hurts.

One of los patos *makes a fatal mistake.*

CHAPTER SEVENTY-TWO

Los Patos

DESPITE ITS STATUS AS A CELESTIAL ICON of exotic locations, I've always found the Southern Cross an oddly indistinct constellation. I've observed it from locations as diverse as the Namibian desert, Tierra del Fuego, and the Great Barrier Reef, but I always have to study the sky to find it, and I'm not always certain when I have. Contrast this ambiguity to the clarity of our familiar Dippers and Orion; even Scorpio, the southernmost of our major Northern hemisphere constellations, seems easy to locate and identify in comparison.

True to form, the Cross remained elusive above the darkened marsh that morning, at least to my eye. But below 32 degrees south latitude it is visible at all times, so I knew it had to be up there somewhere. "I think I see it," I finally said to Lori without much conviction.

"Maybe you should stop stargazing and look over there," she suggested.

Far across the *pampas* the sunrise was still little more than a dull bulge of light beneath the horizon, but waves of ducks had started to rise from the sea of reeds, filling the backlit sky with countless dots that slowly coalesced into shimmering curtains. In 60 years of duck hunting, I'd never seen anything quite like it.

The wind was dead calm, and our decoys, silhouetted against the polished surface of the lake, looked more like a still life painting than a flock of ducks. But in all probability the birds rising from the reeds had never been hunted before, and they didn't care. Moments later, the first set of the morning pitched into the spread while I stood motionless and watched.

Before dropping us off with a supply of shotgun shells that would have lasted me for weeks back home, our host had assured us that there was no such thing as legal shooting light in Argentina and that we were free to open up whenever we felt like it, but I didn't yet, for several reasons. I'd studied my bird book the night before, but it was still too dark for me to know what I was shooting at. Although plainly visible against the eastern sky, inbound birds disappeared completely when they dropped below the level of the reeds, making them impossible to track. Finally, old habits of restraint die hard in any legal jurisdiction, and I already knew that plenty of shooting lay ahead.

After watching the show in silence for another 20 minutes, a flock of yellow-billed pintails finally made me an offer I couldn't refuse. Bowhunting was the primary purpose of the trip and I hadn't felt like lugging one of my own shotguns to Argentina, so I was carrying a borrowed autoloader that felt heavy and awkward in my hands. At least that's the excuse I'm invoking to explain why just one bird lay in the decoys by the time the marsh fell silent once again.

No matter. The show was just beginning.

The outdoor writing life has provided me with plenty of excuses to travel widely about the world, and I've encountered a fascinating array of waterfowl in the process. The *sine qua non*, of course, is habitat, primarily defined by water. Provide it, to paraphrase Kevin Costner's character in *Field of Dreams*, and they will come, as I learned in regions as diverse as the South Pacific, sub-Saharan Africa, and Siberia.

During those travels, waterfowl species familiar from home often turned up in unexpected places. Most North American waterfowl enjoy a circumpolar distribution, which explains my sense of *déjà vu* when I encountered harlequins and green-winged teal trading up and down remote Russian rivers. Sportsmen deliberately introduced some of our favorites elsewhere, hence the mallard's presence in Australia. Parallel evolution has led to some remarkable waterfowl look-alikes around the globe, which is why there's a Cape shoveler in southern Africa and an Australasian shoveler in the South Pacific that bear a remarkable resemblance to our own spoonbill even though they are distinct species.

But waterfowl disperse along lines of longitude as well as latitude, as a flock of teal reminded me that morning in Argentina. The birds flared directly overhead as I rose to shoot, and the lead drake fell right into the blind with us. And there it was: a *colorado* to our Argentine friends but a cinnamon teal to us, one of the most beautiful and less frequently encountered puddle ducks on the Montana prairie. Hard to believe I had to go all the way across the equator to find the first one I'd seen in years.

We shot a lot of ducks that morning, by our standards if not by those of our hosts. But the "high volume" aspect of typical Argentine wing-shooting has never held much appeal for me, and I frankly recoil whenever I see a mountain of dead doves in a grain field no matter how much trouble they ostensibly cause local farmers. Because of the way I was raised, it was important to me that the birds we killed that morning come to an honorable conclusion.

And so I supervised the field dressing and made sure the delightfully varied bag mad it back to the hacienda with us. After returning home empty-handed from our evening bowhunt, I butted my way into the kitchen, befriended the chef, and made a number of largely irrelevant suggestions in my inelegant Spanish, helped along by several shared glasses of splendid malbec bottled on site by our host.

Argentine society, perhaps the most admirable of any I've encountered in my travels, is based on vast enthusiasm for many of the best things in life including food, music, conversation, outdoor sport, family, and wine. Even by this high standard our table seemed particularly lively that night, with the banter focused largely upon the appreciation of waterfowl, both in the field and on the table. In accordance with local custom, the meal lasted well into the wee hours, which no doubt shifted the following morning's odds considerably in favor of the red deer.

So, *a los patos*!

TJ Conrads hauls a late season limit through the snow.

CHAPTER SEVENTY-THREE

Closing Days

LOW IN THE SOUTHWESTERN SKY the sun was trying to provide warmth and illumination, but that was an exercise in futility. A simple diagram showing the way the earth's axis tips in relation to its orbital path as the seasons progress would have made the phenomenon easy to explain, but it was still hard to believe that this was the same sun that had baked the prairie relentlessly six months earlier. Of course with the winter solstice two weeks past the days were getting longer, but they had a long way to go.

I hadn't had the courage to look at the thermometer when I left the house, but I knew it was cold enough to make my breath turn to ice the moment I stepped out of the truck. The dogs didn't care, and I felt their enthusiasm lift my spirits when they hit the ground frolicking like puppies. Cold seems to stimulate Labrador retrievers the way heat stimulates snakes, especially when they know they're going hunting. Whatever consideration I might have given to turning around and going home couldn't have survived the eager looks Kenai and Rocky offered as I shouldered the decoy bag and headed for the creek.

A fair weather hunter—that is to say, a hunter whose enthusiasm doesn't overwhelm her common sense—Lori had elected to stay behind that afternoon. Hunting by myself, I didn't really need both dogs. But it was the last day of the season, and they needed closure just as badly as I did. Since they'd spent their season soaking wet while I'd been warm and dry, they probably deserved it even more.

The foot of snow that had fallen gently the night before was cold enough to squeak underfoot as I made my way through the willows. Suddenly Kenai flushed a rooster from a patch of frozen cattails. I reflexively dropped the decoy bag and shifted my feet for a shot that never came, since pheasant season had closed the week before. After praising Kenai for a job well done, I continued on toward the dense ribbon of ice fog marking the creek's course ahead.

When I finally arrived at the familiar backwater, I paused. Throwing the decoys into the eddy would obligate me to get them back out at some point, a cold and nasty task. Did two more hours of duck hunting at the end of a long season justify the effort?

I answered my own question by tossing the blocks into the stream and settling back against an old cottonwood log to wait.

Opening days are the ones that everyone marks on their calendar. I'm not going to argue against that practice. Back when I was a kid, the opening days of various seasons meant even more to me than conventional holidays, my birthday, and the last day of school, and things haven't changed much since. But in its own way the last day of the season is as significant as the first, and it deserves more attention than it gets.

There are certainly reasons to ignore it. The weather is often better suited to fireplaces than duck blinds, especially in Alaska and Montana where I've lived my adult life. The freezer may be full, and even if it isn't the thought of plucking one more duck with frozen fingers may be too much to bear. And if you spend as much time outdoors as I do, you may feel just plain tired, a phenomenon that only increases with age.

But whenever I find myself about to yield to such rationalizations, all I have to do is stop and think about how long it will be before I get to do it again. Confronting that grim reality is usually all it takes to get me pulling on long underwear, removing the shotgun from the cabinet, and heading toward the kennel no matter what the weather.

Back on the creek, I'm engaged in a mental exercise learned during long hours of patient waiting while carrying my longbow in the field: letting my surroundings become as close as possible to what they would be if I wasn't there. I suppose this process is a form of meditation, but I just want to appreciate the subtle sounds of the winter birdlife and the soothing rhythm of the current passing by. However, the Labs are busy being Labs, and by the third time Kenai has crawled up into my lap, I've given up.

Just in the nick of time, as events soon prove. As soon as I've risen to stamp my feet against the cold I notice both dogs' attention focused downstream, and suddenly there's a lone duck descending toward the decoys. The bird is a mallard—at this time of year I wouldn't expect anything else—but despite the close range the flat light makes me hesitate for a moment while I confirm its gender. Even though this could be my last duck of the season, I don't want it badly enough to kill a hen.

Then the bird turns into the feeble sunlight and all the right cues register. The shot itself is kid stuff. I don't even bother issuing commands to the dogs as the kicking drake bobs away on the current. This may be their last dance too, and as far as I'm concerned they can make the retrieve together.

The race goes to the young, and moments later Kenai delivers the bird to my outstretched hand while I console Rocky with credit for an assist. Then I declare the season over and brace myself for the struggle with the icy decoy lines. Paying homage to closing day has never required killing a limit of ducks. Like reading the last chapter of a good book, it's a way to summarize all that has gone before and bring it to a proper conclusion.

Darkness is falling by the time I head to the truck… and the long wait until next season.

Don and Rocky at the end of another season.

Ducks Unlimited

NONE OF THIS WOULD HAVE BEEN POSSIBLE without Ducks Unlimited.

And I do mean none of it: not the book, not the columns, none of the myriad experiences and observations recorded over the course of six decades afield in the company of waterfowl.

I'm hardly the only outdoors enthusiast who owes a debt of gratitude to Ducks Unlimited, or DU as it is commonly known in waterfowl circles. Founded and sustained by hunters, DU's prime beneficiaries obviously derive from the ranks of the millions who head to the field each fall with shotguns and retrievers intent upon enjoying just the kind of experiences I have chronicled in this volume.

Except—and this is a key point—that this "obvious" assumption doesn't stand up to scrutiny. While hunters deserve credit for salvaging North American waterfowl populations from the brink of destruction, the birds are here today for all of us to enjoy, whether we choose to do so with a shotgun, a camera, or a pair of binoculars. I have examined the regrettable rift between hunters and the non- (or outright anti-) hunting segments of the wildlife advocacy community in detail elsewhere (*How Sportsmen Saved the World*: Lyons Press, 2010). I still challenge members of the second group to name a non-hunting organization that has done as much for North American wildlife and habitat as DU.

Since its founding in 1937, when continental waterfowl populations had reached a nadir that could well have precluded their recovery, DU has lobbied Congress, helped draft key legislation, and educated hunting and non-hunting segments of the public alike. The organization has raised hundreds of millions of dollars for waterfowl (some 90% of which goes directly into wildlife habitat) and sponsored thousands of wetlands restoration projects (which benefit countless non-game species as well as the ducks and geese we hunt every year.)

Beyond question, the most contentious wildlife issue I've ever faced has been the reintroduction of the grey wolf to the Rocky Mountain States, an effort characterized by endless rounds of divisive litigation that consumed millions of dollars that could have been used more wisely for the benefit of wildlife in other ways. No matter how one feels about wolves in Montana, Idaho, and Wyoming, this bitter experience should have taught us all that lawsuits and rational wildlife management seldom go together. As if to prove the point, I would remind readers that DU has managed over six decades of successful wildlife advocacy without ever suing anybody.

These brief notes remind me that I could write an entire book about Ducks Unlimited and its accomplishments, and perhaps someday I will. For now, I'll have to settle for lauding the central role this organization has played in everything described between these covers. Since you're reading this book, chances are excellent that you are already a DU supporter. If you are, please consider this a gentle reminder to renew your membership, attend your local banquet, educate others about DU and its mission, and write DU an extra check at the end of the season. And if you're not, you should be. Contact: Ducks Unlimited, One Waterfowl Way Memphis, TN 38120.

About the Cover Artist

FOR YEARS NOW, Bob White's evocative paintings have been as much a part of the back page columns in *Ducks Unlimited* as my own writing. It is a privilege to have an example of Bob's work on this book's cover.

Bob officially regards his career as an expression of a "misspent youth", as do I. The antithesis of an aesthete, Bob spends his summers guiding anglers in Southwest Alaska, and his art reflects the perspective of an outdoorsman who has "been there, done that." He traces his artistic influences back to Homer and Sargent, to whose work his own demands serious comparison. It has been an honor to work with him.

To learn more, visit the website www.bobwhitestudio.com.

About the Author

DON THOMAS writes regularly about bowhunting, wing-shooting, fly-fishing, and wildlife for numerous outdoor publications and has authored 17 books on related subjects. He serves as co-editor of *Traditional Bowhunter Mgazine*, Editor-at-Large for *Retriever Journal*, and Field Editor for *Ducks Unlimited*, and writes regular columns for *Bowhunter* and *Salmon and Steelhead Journal*. His work also appears regularly in publications such as *Gray's Sporting Journal*, *Alaska Magazine*, *Fish Alaska*, *Pheasants Forever*, *Shooting Sportsman*, and *Big Sky Journal*. He works part time as a physician on a remote Montana Indian reservation and as a bear hunting guide in Alaska, where he has also been a pilot and commercial fisherman. He and his wife Lori divide their time between homes in rural Montana and coastal Alaska. Hounds, bird dogs, and Labrador retrievers have largely taken the place of their four grown children.

Designer

ELLE JAY DESIGN

Lindsay J. Nyquist

www.ellejaydesign.com

books
brochures
business cards
letterhead
newsletters
and just about anything else

Press

RAVEN'S EYE PRESS
Rediscovering the West
www.ravenseyepress.com

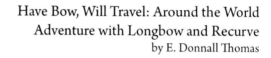

Have Bow, Will Travel: Around the World
Adventure with Longbow and Recurve
by E. Donnall Thomas

Racks: A Natural History of
Antlers and the Animals That
Wear Them
by David Petersen

Ghost Grizzlies: Does the Great
Bear Still Haunt Colorado?
by David Petersen

Heartsblood: Hunting,
Spirituality, and Wildness in
America
by David Petersen

The Monkey Wrench Dad: Dispatches from
the Backyard Frontline
by Ken Wright

COMING FALL 2011
Longbow: A Hardhunting Life, by Jay Campbell

Visit www.ravenseyepress.com
for a complete listing of our titles.

CPSIA information can be obtained at www.ICGtesting.com
Printed in the USA
BVOW031350190911

271437BV00002B/1/P